MARTIN LUTHER KING JR.

A King Family Tribute

By **ANGELA FARRIS WATKINS**

Foreword by **ANDREW YOUNG**

Abrams, New York

Editor: Howard Reeves
Designer: Rogers Eckersly Design
Production Manager: Alison Gervais

Library of Congress Cataloging-in-Publication Data:

Watkins, Angela Farris.
Martin Luther King Jr. : a King family tribute / edited by Angela Farris Watkins.
     p. cm.
  Includes bibliographical references and index.
  ISBN 978-1-4197-0269-3 (alk. paper)
1. King, Martin Luther, Jr., 1899-1984. 2. King, Martin Luther, Jr.,
1929-1968—Family. 3. African American civil rights workers—Biography.
4. African American leadership—History—20th century. 5. African
Americans—Civil rights—History—20th century. 6. Civil rights
Movements—United States—History—20th century. I. Title.
  E185.97.K5W325 2012
  323.092—dc23
  [B]
                    2012008320

Note: Many of the photographs reproduced in this book are in pristine condition, while others are torn and frayed, even copies of copies of originals long lost to griefs. Further, casual photographs taken in the first part of the twentieth century have not held up well to the test of time. But all the photographs in this book are treasured keepsakes of the King family, shared with us as a whole for the first time.

Printed and bound in China
10 9 8 7 6 5 4 3 2 1

Abrams books are available at special discounts when purchased in quantity for premiums and promotions as well as fundraising or educational use. Special editions can also be created to specification. For details, contact specialsales@abramsbooks.com or the address below.

115 West 18th Street
New York, NY 10011
www.abramsbooks.com

To the generations of Kings; now living, before, and evermore.

With gratitude to Almighty God. May faith, hope, and love abide!

Martin Jr. and his sister Christine in 1930.

CONTENTS

❦

FOREWORD

Martin Luther King Jr. was a global phenomenon. He dreamed a new world but also spent twenty of his thirty-nine years making it a reality for citizens from the American South, as well as for those around the world.

The monument for Martin Luther King Jr. on the National Mall in Washington, DC, is a testament to his life and vision. But what causes such greatness? How do some men emerge and tower over history while most of us become merely victims of our life circumstances?

It is important to have some understanding and insight into the childhood and youth of this monumental personality. No one can better supply those insights than members of his own family.

Of course, family members are prone to point out those special signs of genius and prophecy, and there's no doubt there were many, now that we are looking back. But who was "ML" the boy? The boy who went to day camp at the Butler Street YMCA, worked in a mattress factory, picked tobacco with other Morehouse students in Connecticut.

Who was the boy of fifteen entering Morehouse College? What did Dr. Benjamin Mays see in him that other professors did not? What kind of son, brother, husband, father, pastor, was he?

I was amazed the first time I saw him on a basketball court or by a pool table speaking nonviolence in Birmingham. He spoke to everyone, always having time for "the least of those God's children." Where did these "manhood skills" come from?

Included here is a special family tribute by Dr. Christine King Farris, the sister of Dr. King and the only surviving member of his childhood home. Only his family can give us the clues to his calling; the boy, the youth, the student, and finally the man among men and the man of God.

Thanks to his family for taking on this challenge.

ANDREW YOUNG

*In these pages you will experience
the love and the struggle that surrounded
Dr. Martin Luther King Jr.
as he developed into a leader of a movement
committed to a just society for all people.
The personal reflections of family and friends
featured here attest to the power of peace and
harmony that he expressed.*

INTRODUCTION

ALTHOUGH "KING OF HEARTS" IS A PHRASE strongly marked all over the world and is particularly powerful in the hand of the player to whom that card is dealt, King of Heart denotes the power that one man had to ignite significant changes in America and inspire generations of world citizens. His last name was King—Martin Luther King Jr.—and he, with heart, led the American Civil Rights movement.

This is a tribute to his life and work composed of the personal reflections of his family and a few close friends. These reflections bear witness to Martin Luther King Jr.'s unshakeable commitment to justice, righteousness, and truth. They highlight his powerful example of love.

Born on January 15, 1929, Martin Luther King Jr. entered a household of freedom fighters and a community of change agents. It was no accident that he became a change agent and freedom fighter for the world. The home into which he was born was headed by those who knew injustice firsthand and who armed themselves with courage, faith in God, and a determination to do something about it.

Martin Luther King Jr.'s maternal great-grandparents, Willie and Lucretia Williams, were former slaves, who lived in Greene County, Georgia. They were the parents of thirteen children, among them a set of twins, Adam Daniel and his sister Eve.

Adam Daniel Williams, grandfather of Martin Luther King Jr., was armed with a covenant relationship with God and forged the idea of a family committed to justice. Martin Luther King Sr., his father, shared that goal. Martin Luther King Jr. grew up in a household with his maternal grandfather, his maternal grandmother, his father, his mother, his aunt Ida (the sister of his maternal grandmother), and his two siblings, so he learned many lessons from them. He saw injustice first hand and developed the same determination and courage that he observed in his father and grandfather as they confronted injustice. Along with these lessons, his mother and grandmother nurtured him in matters of the heart, the importance of believing in himself and not exchanging hatred for justice.

Adam Daniel Williams left Greene County for Atlanta, where he made the crossing into education as a vehicle for advancement and for achieving his dreams of a better life. He graduated from Atlanta Baptist College in 1898 (it was later rechartered as Morehouse College). With an eye toward improving the lives of other African Americans, he became the second pastor in the history of Ebenezer Baptist Church and proved to be a civil rights advocate for his community. He was the founder of the Atlanta Chapter of the National Association for the Advancement of Colored People and helped to lead the effort that resulted in the opening of Atlanta's first high school for African Americans (Booker T. Washington High School), later attended by his grandson, Martin Luther King Jr.

Adam Daniel Williams married Jennie Celeste Parks in 1899, and they had three children, two of whom died as infants. Alberta Christine, their only surviving child, was educated at Spelman Seminary (later Spelman College), Hampton University, and Morris Brown College. A very talented musician, she served as pianist and organist at her father's church for many, many years. She later bore a child who would change the world. Like her son Martin Jr., she became a martyr for Civil Rights: She was gunned down in Ebenezer Baptist Church on a Sunday morning in June 1974 as she played the organ.

Mike King (who would later change his name to Martin Luther King Sr.) was born toward the end of 1899 on a plantation near Stockbridge, Georgia. He was the son of James and Delia King and as an adult became a preacher. He always had dreams of preaching in a large church, so in pursuit of that goal, and motivated by the frustrations of sharecropping, King walked to Atlanta. There, Adam Daniel Williams befriended him and became his mentor. Williams made it clear that King had to get an education and encouraged him as he entered Morehouse College, from which he graduated with a bachelor of arts degree. Later he would serve on its Board of Trustees.

Mike King married Williams's daughter, Alberta, and they had three children together: Willie Christine, Martin Jr., and Alfred Daniel. Later, at the request of his own father, James Albert King, Mike King eventually changed his name to Martin Luther King, Sr. and his son's to Martin Luther King, Jr. James King had insisted that he was supposed to be named after James' two brothers, Martin and Luther. After a time, when Williams died in 1931, King took over the pastorate of Ebenezer Baptist Church. Like his mentor and father-in-law, Martin Luther King Sr. also advocated for social justice. He led local voting rights protests and was responsible for spearheading the actions that led to the equalization of African American teachers' salaries with those of white teachers.

The Williams-King family filled the pulpit at Ebenezer until the retirement of the elder King in 1975, the year after the assassination of his wife in the heritage sanctuary of the church.

In these pages you will experience the love and the struggle that surrounded Dr. Martin Luther King Jr. as he developed into a leader of a movement committed to a just society for all people. The personal reflections of family and friends featured here attest to the power of peace and harmony that he expressed.

In a very real sense, this book symbolizes the instinctive spirit of peace and harmony that God places within each human being. As we honor our beloved Martin, we renew our commitment to the greater pilgrimage of peace and harmony that led Adam Daniel Williams to leave Greene County, Mike King to leave Stockbridge, and Martin Luther King Jr. to become a drum major for justice.

CHAPTER 1

BORN FOR THIS

MARTIN LUTHER KING SR.

Father

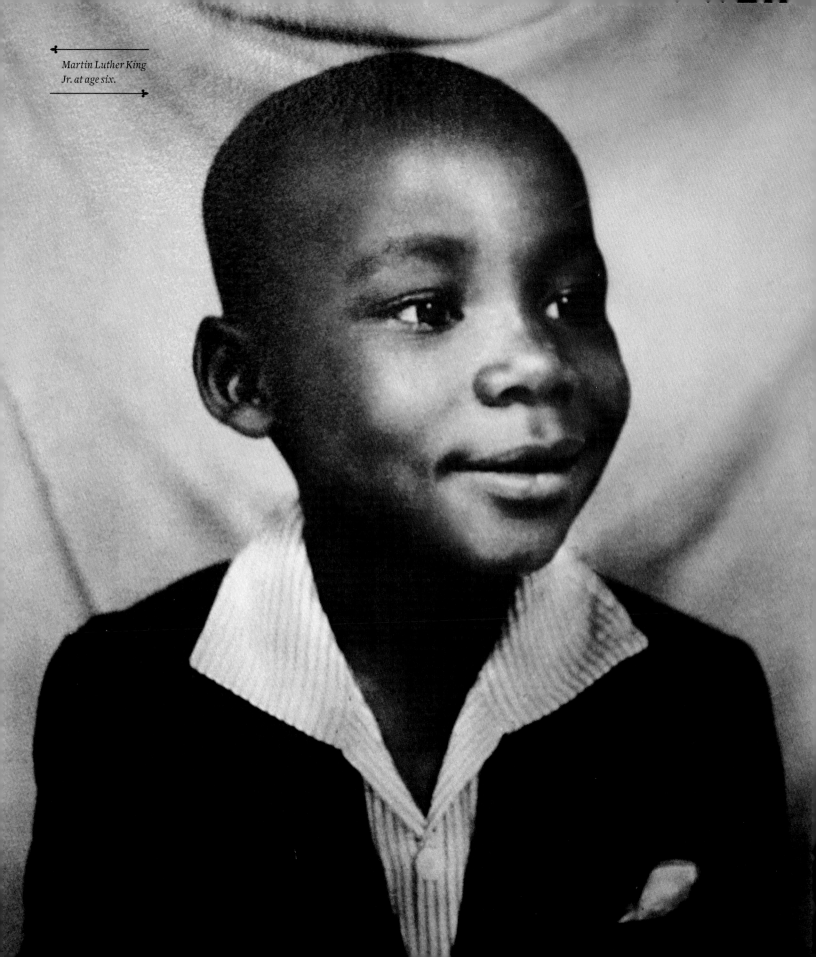

Martin Luther King Jr. was born into a family of leaders and change agents who nurtured him in a spirit of love and expected him to continue their legacy of social justice.

WHEN ML WAS SIX YEARS OLD, I took him downtown with me, and we enjoyed a very pleasant ride in the family car. In those days we seldom shopped outside the Negro business community, but on one of the bigger streets near the center of town, ML spotted a pair of shoes in a window and asked me to buy them. Well, he needed a pair, and so we went inside the store where the shoes he liked so much were displayed. A clerk appeared as soon as we stepped past the door and very coldly announced that we should go to the back of the store where he'd help us in just a few minutes. I told him we were quite comfortable in the front of the store, and if he didn't want to sell us any shoes there, we wouldn't be buying any.

This was the ridiculous nature of segregation in the South. A grown man could make no sense of it to a very bright six-year-old boy. ML just couldn't understand why it was all right to buy shoes in the back part of a store and not in the front. Because people come in so many different colors in the Negro community, it was hard for him to figure out how anybody could use the color of a person's skin to separate him from others.

ML stared at me in the car and asked me to explain the whole thing again. And I said to him that the best way to explain it was to say that I'd never accept the stupidity and cruelty of segregation, not as long as I lived. I was going to be fighting against it in some way or other as long as there was breath in me. I wanted him to understand *that*. He still looked puzzled. But he nodded his head and told me that if I was against it, he would help me all he could. And I remember smiling and telling him how much I appreciated his support.

He was such a little fellow then, but sitting there next to me in the car, ML seemed so thoughtful and determined on this matter that I felt certain he wouldn't forget his promise to help.

ML . . . was a great speaker as a young boy, and he sang, too, in a fine, clear voice. His schoolwork, in both the private and public institutions he attended, was always of a high caliber. And he loved church, in a way I could recall in myself: the feeling for ceremonies and ritual, the passionate love of Baptist music.

Perhaps it was a sign of the impatience that was coming that ML decided to skip his final year at Washington High School and enter Morehouse College as a fifteen-year-old freshman. In a way both distant and close to my decision at that age to go off and become rich working on the railroad, my son had decided to reach higher.

Nineteen sixty—a new decade, and another beginning for me. I was happy—ML was coming back to Atlanta. At the end of each phase of education, I had tried to get him to join me in the pulpit at Ebenezer, but ML had always listened politely and patiently to my arguments and said, "No, Dad, not yet." Now he and Coretta had spent five years at Dexter [Dexter Avenue Baptist Church, Montgomery, Alabama]. They had enjoyed a beautiful and fulfilling experience in their first pastorate, and I thanked God for that. ML had successfully led the Montgomery Bus Boycott, which began as a local issue and drew national, then international attention. It also spawned other bus boycotts in the South, which led a group of clergy in 1957 to the founding of the Southern Christian Leadership Conference. ML was elected president of SCLC, having no idea that the demands and responsibilities of the organization would increase as quickly as they did.

Now it was a matter of living with him in this commitment. Clearly, the issue was no longer just a bus company in Montgomery. There was bound to be more. And nobody could really predict just how far whites would go to try to stop what was now becoming a mass movement drawing attention from around the world. It was the beginning of many unhappy, anxious hours we would spend, Bunch [Alberta King] and I, waiting for word, hoping that no madman had found a way to ML's door. But we could only support what he chose to do. Bunch often said that she would never fail to stand with him, though she was not always in agreement with the ways the movement chose to accomplish its work. But she'd grown up in her father's house, hearing him preach and plan as he sought to bring about the fall of Southern segregation. So, of course, she knew it was useless to try to persuade others to do what ML had now learned he was most capable of doing: providing leadership when it was clearly needed.

His preaching was rich with spirit and power. He could move people with great, rolling thunder in his voice, the words moving smoothly from him and reaching people with the enormous conviction that all speakers who can move masses of human beings bring to the simplest sentence. He was becoming a national leader because it was time for this to happen, and time, of course, for it to happen to Martin Luther King Jr.

MARTIN LUTHER KING SR.

Father

(excerpted from Daddy King: An Autobiography, *1980)*

Jennie Celeste Williams, maternal grandmother of Martin Luther King Jr.

Opposite: Rev. Adam Daniel Williams, maternal grandfather of Martin Luther King Jr.

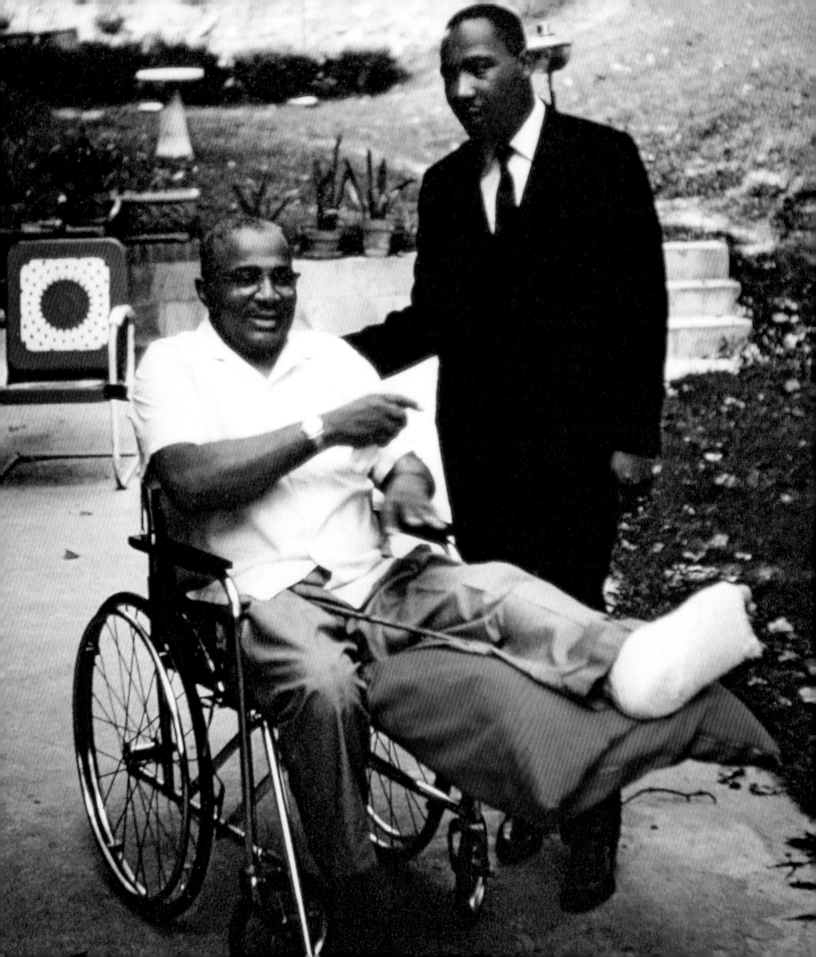

In Martin Luther King Sr.'s office at Ebenezer Baptist Church, Atlanta, on the occasion of Martin Jr.'s first book release (Stride Toward Freedom). Seated left to right: Martin Jr.; Alberta Williams King; Martin Sr.; Martin Jr.'s sister, Christine; and his brother, Alfred Daniel.

CHAPTER 2

REFLECTIONS OF A MOTHER'S LOVE

ALBERTA WILLIAMS KING

Mother

Martin Jr. with his mother, Alberta Williams King, in the backyard of his parents' Northwest Atlanta home.

Sunday Night
10:30

Dear Mother,

Your letter was received this morning. I often tell the boys around the campus I have the best mother in the world. You will never know how I appreciate the many kind things you and daddy are doing for me. So far I have gotten the money ($ dollars) every week.

As to my wanting some clippings from the newspapers, I must answer yes. I wondered why you hadn't sent many, especially the Atlanta world.

You stated that my letters aren't newsy enough. Well

2

I don't have much news. I never go anywhere much but in these books. Sometimes the professor comes in class and tells us to read our assignments in Hebrew, and that is really hard.

Do you know the girl I used to date at Spelman (Gloria Royster). She is in school at Temple and I have been to see her twice. Also I met a fine chick in Phila who has gone over the old boy. Since Barbour tell the members of his church that my family were rich, the girls are running me down. Of course, I don't ever think about them. I am too busy studying.

3

I eat dinner at Barbour's home quite often. He is full of fury, and he has one of the best minds of anybody I have ever met.

I haven't had time to contact any of your friends up this way. Maybe I will get to it pretty soon.

I hope you will explain to the members why I haven't written any of them. I am going to write a letter to the entire church next week. It should be there

4

by the first Sunday.

I hear from Christine every week. I try to answer her as regularly as possible. I hope she will somehow get adjusted to that accounting.

Rev. Ray was there Friday at the state convention. He told me to come up anytime I get ready. He is looking for you and dad in November.

Well I guess I must go back to studying. Give everybody my Regards.

Your son
"M.L."

In October 1948, just after Martin Luther King Jr. entered Crozer Theological Seminary, he wrote to his mother in response to a letter that she had written to him. Their closeness is apparent in the subjects he discusses with her.

Sunday Night
10:30

Dear Mother,

Your letter was received this morning. I often tell the boys around the campus I have the best mother in the world. You will never know how I appreciate the many kind thing[s] you and [D]addy are doing for me. So far I have gotten the money (5 dollars) every week.

As to my wanting some clippings from the newspapers, I must answer yes. I wondered why you hadn't sent many, especially the Atlanta world.

You stated that my letters aren't newsy enough. Well I don't have much news. I never go anywhere much but in these books. Some times the professor comes in class and tells us to read out assignments in Hebrew, and that is really hard.

Do you know the girl I used to date at Spelman (Gloria Royster). She is in school at Temple and I have been to see her twice. Also I met a fine chick in Phila[delphia] who had gone wild over the old boy. Since Barbor told the members of his church that my family was rich, the girls are running me down. Of course, I don't ever think about them I am to[o] busy studying.

I eat dinner at Barbor[']s house quite often. He is full of fun, and he has one of the best minds of anybody I have ever met.

I haven't had time to contact any of your friends up this way. Maybe I will get to it pretty soon.

I hope you will explain to the members why I haven't written any of them. I am going to write a letter to the entire church next week. It should be there by the first Sunday.

I hear from Christine every week. I try to answer her as regularly as possible. I hope she will somehow get adjusted to that accounting.

Rev. Ray was here Friday at the state convention. He told me to come up anytime I get ready. He is looking for you and [D]ad in November.

Well I guess I must go back to studying. Give everybody my Regards.

Your son,
"ML"

The King family, shortly after Christmas. The children are wearing some of the clothes they were given as presents. Pictured from left to right: Bottom row: Alfred Daniel, Christine, Martin Jr. Top row: Alberta Williams King, Martin Sr., the children's grandmother Jennie Celeste Williams. (Year unknown)

A graduation
reception for the
King children, 1948.
Left to right: Alfred
Daniel, from Palmer
Memorial Institute
(high school);
Christine, from
Spelman College;
Martin Jr., from
Morehouse College;
Alberta Williams
King; Martin Sr.

Opposite:
Martin Jr. and
Christine in 1930.

CHAPTER 3

EXPRESSIONS FROM A LOVING SISTER

CHRISTINE KING FARRIS

Sister

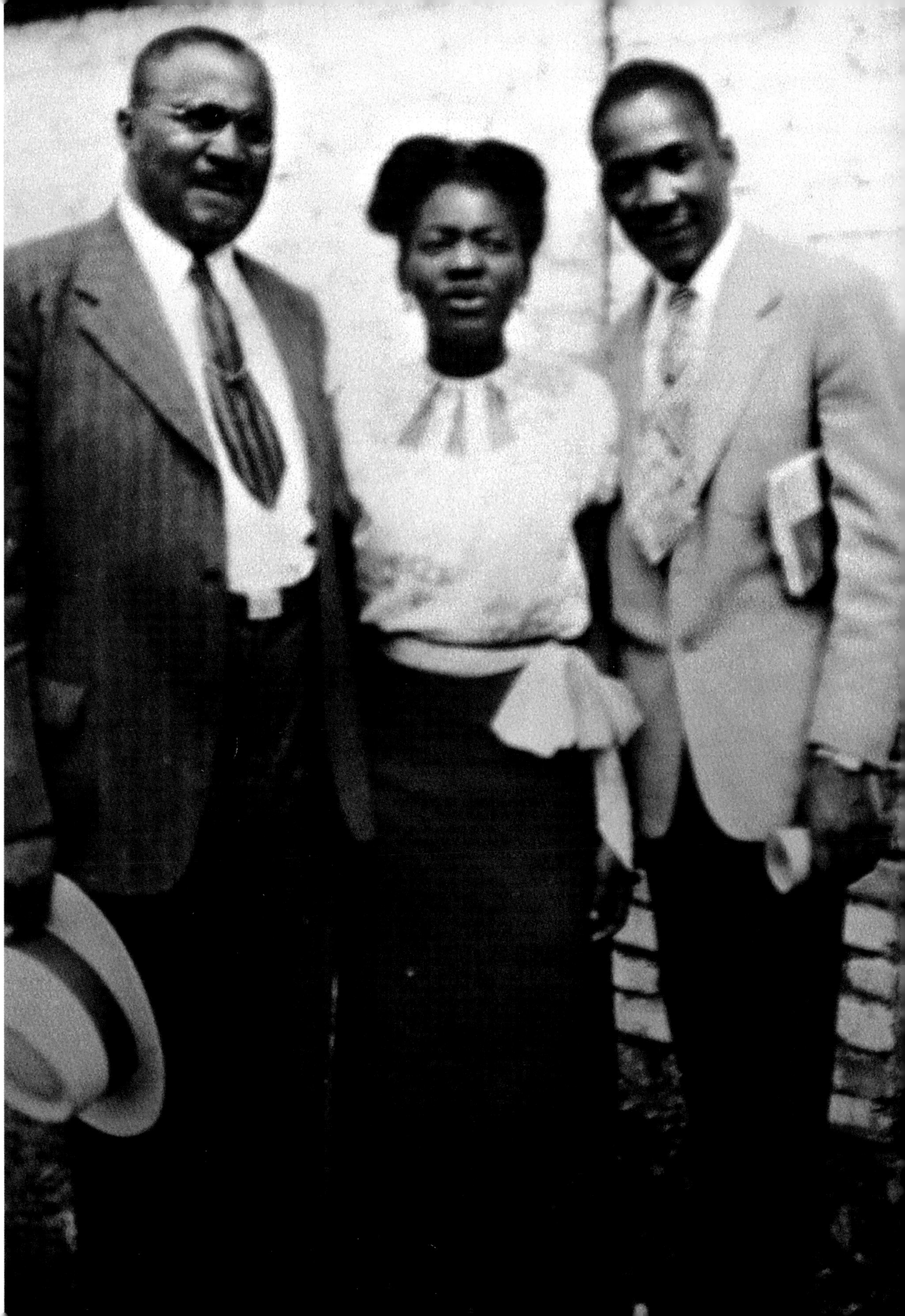

*Martin Sr.,
Christine,
and Martin Jr.*

The only surviving member of the household into which Martin Luther King Jr. was born reflects on what it was like growing up with him.

MARTIN AND I had a normal brother-sister relationship, with lots of affection. As youngsters, we sometimes gave each other a hard time, like sisters and brothers everywhere. I remember, for example, Martin and our brother, AD, pulling the heads off my dolls to aggravate me. But the teasing and mischief rarely got out of hand, because our father and mother ran a pretty tight ship.

But we were very close. Martin said that he decided to be baptized after he saw me being baptized. And even as we grew into teenagers, we shared many of our confidences, hopes, and dreams for the future.

Martin also wanted to follow behind me when I registered at Young Street Elementary School. Mother took Martin along. He was only five years old, and the requirement was that you had to be six years old. He wanted to start school so bad that my mother agreed to register him. He was later sent back home after he remarked to his classmates that he had celebrated a birthday and there were five candles on his cake, and the teacher overheard him. So he returned as soon as he turned six years old. I guess he made up for it later with his early admittance to college.

Martin showed leadership skills early on, and as a teenager, he was already revealing that he had a creative approach to problem solving and a seriousness about social problems you didn't find in many young men his age. He was a visionary even as a very young man. Long before he was a leader, I think he had a deeply felt dream of the Beloved Community, a concept he envisioned where people would work and live together, no matter their differences. There was something inside him that could not accept injustice, a voice that urged him to seek a better way.

Martin was already a truth seeker by the time he went to college at the age of fifteen. He enjoyed his social life at Morehouse and later at Crozer Theological Seminary and then Boston University—he was a good dancer and a snappy dresser who liked a good party as much as any of his fellow students. But at the same time, he took on his studies with a focused seriousness. He read the Bible, the great philosophers, and theologians with determination, not just to get good grades, but to understand their teachings and do something with what he learned.

There were many exciting times during our college days. Martin was at Morehouse College, and I was just across the street at Spelman College. When he entered college early, we ended up in the same class year. During our senior year, Martin gave his trial sermon. I got permission to leave campus so that I could hear him. (In those days you were carefully monitored. I had to get permission.) It was at our church, Ebenezer Baptist Church.

I remember that before Martin spoke, he met with a group of ministers that asked him many questions about his call to the ministry. Then he came out and delivered his first sermon to the congregation. I remember like it was yesterday. He had on a dark suit with a white shirt and a tie. I was anxious for him, praying that it would turn out fine, and of course it did. It was very well received. He did a great job!

At Crozer Theological Seminary, near Philadelphia, Martin had his first exposure to the teachings of Mahatma Gandhi in an extracurricular lecture he attended. My brother later wrote that the lecture, delivered by Professor Mordecai Johnson, who had recently visited India, "electrified" him with a growing awareness. It would later bear fruit in Montgomery, Alabama, when Martin first became leader of the Civil Rights Movement and used some of Gandhi's tactics and philosophy. He later would write that "Christ furnished the spirit and motivation, while Gandhi furnished the method" of the Civil Rights Movement.

When he went to Boston University to work on a doctorate, I went to Columbia University to work on a graduate degree also. I remember the times we visited with each other on our campuses. Once when I went to visit him, he wanted me to meet this young lady that he had been telling me about. We picked her up and went to dinner. Her name was Coretta Scott. She was nice and very attractive. Later, Martin told Mother and Dad that he was getting ready to be engaged. When I realized that Martin didn't have money to buy her engagement ring, I gave him the money. We were close like that. He wasn't working then. I was working as a schoolteacher and had a little to spare.

I am often asked what my brother was like as a person. It's a fair question, since I knew him longer than anyone who is now alive. Martin was truly a delightful person at the human level. He loved people, and he had the ability to make everyone feel good when they were with him. He had a great sense of humor, and he loved to make people laugh.

He was also what you could call a "regular guy" in the way he related to people. He was completely unpretentious—he didn't act any different toward people after he won the Nobel Peace Prize. He would often stop and chat with people in the community on Auburn Avenue outside his office. He was not only a good talker, but a good listener, and anyone could come to him with a problem and he would do what he could to help.

My brother did not consciously plan to be a great civil rights leader. In fact, you could say he was drafted into that role when he was elected president of the Montgomery Improvement Association in 1955.

I would like everyone to understand that Martin Luther King Jr. was a man of action, a leader who was determined not only to win freedom for his people, but to win freedom, not with violence, not with threats, but with love—unconditional love for all people, accepting them just as they are, respecting their personhood, even if you deplore their behavior. He believed that every person, no matter how misguided, is a child of God and deserves your respect and your compassion.

And so I call on everyone who reveres Martin's legacy to march on with us to the promised land, with unconditional love, a radiant faith in nonviolence, and a vision of the Beloved Community. With this commitment, let us carry forward into the twenty-first century the living spirit of Martin Luther King Jr., whose example and legacy sustain and nourish our hopes for justice, peace, and unity.

CHRISTINE KING FARRIS
Sister

Martin Jr. (at almost one year of age) and Christine (at just over two years of age) with their father, in the front yard of their family home in Atlanta.

Opposite: Martin Jr. and Christine as toddlers, in the driveway of their Atlanta home.

CHAPTER 4

BELOVED BROTHERS

ALFRED DANIEL WILLIAMS KING
Brother

Alfred Daniel and Martin Jr. relaxing against Martin Jr.'s car, outside the Atlanta home of another member of the Ebenezer Baptist Church.

Martin Jr. and Alfred Daniel, with their schoolbooks, in front of their childhood home in Atlanta.

Alfred Daniel Williams King, Martin Luther King Jr.'s only brother, was a minister of the gospel and fully supportive of Martin Jr.'s work. They shared a brotherhood of love and laughter, hardships and courage. Alfred Daniel served by his brother's side in the struggle for equality.

Martin Luther King Jr. believed in nonviolence. He did love his neighbor as himself. Because he was mortal, this belief was not a gift. It was a philosophy which grew from study, self-discipline, and prayer. As he achieved this way of life, so can I, and so can we all.

REV. ALFRED DANIEL WILLIAMS KING

Brother
(excerpt from press statement shortly after the death of Martin Luther King Jr., April 1968)

CHAPTER 5

MEMORIES OF A COLLEGE CLASSMATE

SAMUEL DUBOIS COOK
Morehouse College Classmate

Martin Luther King Jr. entered Morehouse College at fifteen years of age and finished with a salute to his graduating class. A college classmate remembers this experience with him.

"ML" IS WHAT WE GENERALLY CALLED HIM during our student days at Morehouse College. Largely because of his abundant oratorical gifts and intellect, ML was selected to deliver the senior class sermon in June of 1948. As expected, he soared and stood tall. I shall never forget one of his compelling and prophetic points. He asserted that there are moral laws in the universe that we cannot ignore without serious consequences, just as there are physical laws in the universe. He thus affirmed, by implication, the unity and continuity of means and ends, the way and the goal. Fully developed later, the idea became a central part of ML's ethical, social, and political vision and philosophy. In combining theology, philosophy, leadership, and social change in the future, Dr. King was unique in human history and culture.

I recall a fond memory of a time after our college days, when ML and Coretta dropped by my house during the Christmas holidays. My wife, Sylvia, and I offered ML some eggnog. I snuck a swig of bourbon into it when he wasn't looking and gave it to him. He tasted it and said, "I don't know what you put in it, but whatever it is, it sure is good." When I admitted that I had added a little something, he laughed and laughed.

As ML became a very visible and noted leader of civil rights, there were many rumors and attacks surrounding him. Once, a citizen of our community, who knew my close relations with ML, mentioned to me that there was a particular rumor about ML. The man suggested that I speak with ML about this. I was very angry that there were such attempts to destroy his credibility and image. It happened that I ran into ML the next day at a meeting. I pulled him aside and mentioned what had been told to me. I explained that I thought people were trying to destroy him and that something should be done about this. He responded with such calmness. He assured me that it was truly a rumor and that everything would be all right. Steeped in religion and philosophy, Dr. King's leadership of the Civil Rights Movement was superb, incomparable, and unique. He was a mighty example of ethical

Father and son after Martin Jr.'s graduation from Morehouse College in spring of 1948.

vision, leadership, integrity, incorruptibility, intelligence, and unswerving commitment to the Kingdom of God.

Alexis de Tocqueville (1805–1859), the great French author of the classic book *Democracy in America,* published in the 1830s, asserted his famous statement, "The great advantage of the Americans is that they have arrived at a state of democracy without having to endure a democratic revolution, and that they are born equal instead of becoming so." The statement is profoundly false. Black Americans were not born free and equal. Indeed, at the time, they were essentially victims of the tragic institution of slavery. The terrible forces of history and culture had to await Martin Luther King Jr. in the mid-twentieth century to lead the civil rights revolution and elevate blacks to a plane of essential constitutional equality and freedom. His tragic and untimely death left to others the supreme responsibility to finish the job.

SAMUEL DUBOIS COOK
Morehouse College Classmate

EXTENDING THE KING FAMILY

NAOMI KING *Sister-in-law*
ISAAC N. FARRIS SR. *Brother-in-law*

The King family grew additional branches when Martin Jr. and his siblings married. Alfred Daniel was the first to take this step when he married Naomi Barber in 1950. Martin Jr. married Coretta Scott in 1953. Christine married Isaac N. Farris in 1960.

Martin Jr. and Coretta Scott were married in 1953 at the home of Coretta's parents in Marion, Alabama. Pictured from left to right: Christine, Alfred Daniel, Betty Ann Hill (a cousin of the Kings), Martin Jr., Naomi Barber King (Alfred Daniel's wife), Coretta, Martin Sr., Edith Scott Bagley (Coretta's sister), Bernice Scott (Coretta's mother), Alberta Williams King, Alveda King (daughter of Alfred Daniel and Naomi), and Obie Scott (Coretta's father).

Coretta and Martin Jr. in the living room of their Atlanta home.

Opposite: Martin Jr. with his first two children and his parents, outside Ebenezer Baptist Church in Atlanta after a morning service. Left to right, Martin Luther King III, Martin Jr., Martin Sr., Yolanda Denise King, Alberta Williams King.

"*Our father was a King . . . not the kind you bowed down to . . .
a King who fought for justice with the shield of prayer and the sword
of nonviolence. . . . One who stood up for millions of men, women,
and children. . . . Not the kind who wore a crown but one who
crowned a movement. . . .*"

YOLANDA KING

*From a speech at the Martin Luther King Memorial groundbreaking,
Washington, DC, November 13, 2006*

Martin Jr. playing ball with his sons, Martin III and Dexter Scott, in the front yard of their home in Atlanta.

Martin Jr. buckling the shoe of his youngest child, Bernice Albertine, in the basement of Ebenezer Baptist Church. Coretta stands in the background among others.

"I have a dream . . . that my four little children will one day . . . be judged by the content of their character."

MARTIN LUTHER KING JR.

Excerpt from "I Have a Dream,"
a speech delivered at the Lincoln Memorial,
Washington, DC, August 28, 1963

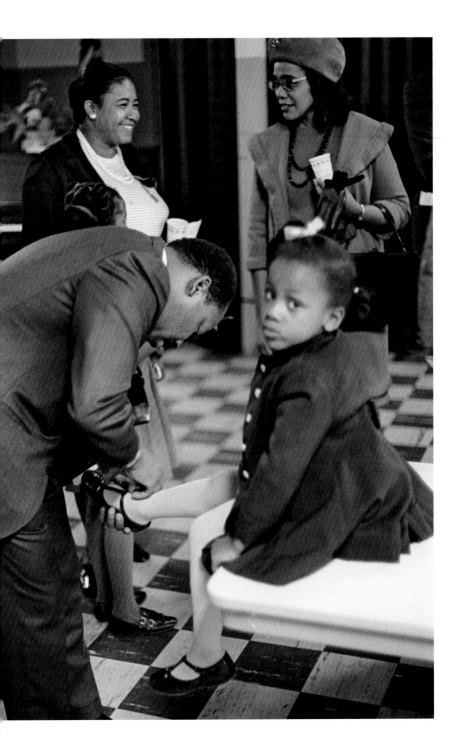

"*People often make comparisons between my way of speaking and my father's. They say that I sound like him.*

I was only five when Daddy was assassinated.... I seldom asked questions about my father.... Suddenly his powerful words mattered to me very much...."

BERNICE A. KING

From Hard Questions, Heart Answers, *1996, Broadway Books*

MET MARTIN when I was a young girl. His brother, AD, wanted to court me. AD and I married, and ML became my brother-in-law. He was truly a giant of a man. He and AD were inseparable. As is often the case in families, we were in and out of each other's lives on many levels. During the tumultuous times of the Civil Rights Movement, ML was the leader and AD was one of ML's top strategists and closest confidants.

I was blessed to have shared abundant living, enjoying the substance and fulfillment of life that came with knowing Dr. Martin Luther King Jr., my devoted brother-in-law. He was a man who loved Almighty God, a husband who dearly adored his wife; he was a father who put his life on the line for his "four little children." ML was also a caring and sharing extended family member who always spent "quality time" with his family. He was a true and sincere minister of the Gospel of Jesus Christ. He shared so much of his life, bestowing love and good works; words cannot truly contain all that he did.

One occasion comes to mind, however. In 1955, I went to Montgomery to spend time with ML and Coretta and their sweet new baby daughter Yolanda. My beautiful niece had been born on my birthday, and she was still a newborn.

While there, I recall sitting on the couch one night in the twilight, waiting for ML to come home. He had been detained at the police station during a demonstration. Coretta was in the back, feeding Yolanda. ML came in the door. His footsteps were heavy, and as he came into the living room, he didn't realize that I was sitting there in the dark.

ML went to the mantel and stood there in the shadows with the light from the street streaming down on his face. He leaned into the mantel and kept running his hand under his collar, working to loosen his tie. As he tugged at the tie, he realized I was sitting there, and he said softly, "Neenie, they choked me with my tie. They choked me so hard that I almost died. But I decided that the more they try to kill me, the more I'll love and forgive them."

No words came from my mouth as I watched my husband's brother standing there tall in the moonlight, armed with the strength to love his enemies.

I can recall another time of strength where we both found a bit of joy and humor in the midst of a dark hour. I received a call from ML just after he was hospitalized in New York after having been stabbed in the chest by a demented woman. He called to let us know how he was doing, and he told me, "Neenie, the doctor says that if I had sneezed, I would have died." I remember saying to him that I was so glad he didn't sneeze. Then he chuckled and said, "I sure wish I had a dish of your sweet potato cobbler, girl." Well, wouldn't you just know it? Coretta was flying up to be with ML in just a few hours, and I had all of the ingredients for my pie right there in the house! I rushed and made the pie, from a secret recipe of my mother. We got the pie to Coretta just as the car taking her to the airport was pulling out of her driveway. The pie was smoking hot, all packed up in a box.

A while later, the phone rang, and it was ML again. He told me that the schoolchildren were sending him letters saying just what I had said—they were all glad that he didn't sneeze. I remember saying that I thank almighty God that you did not sneeze, and I pray for your healing! ML thanked me. Then, I heard him smack his lips. "Girl," he said, "this pie is still hot. What am I going to do with you?"

There are so many memories like this, and there is so little time to share. I can tell you this: Martin Luther King Jr. is sorely missed. May we as brothers and sisters in Christ give God all the glory, honor, love, praise, and thanks for our abundant living, and his gift of this man who was a beloved son, brother, father, preacher, and warrior. He walked in love, and he is truly missed.

NAOMI KING
Sister-in-law

In 1950, at the wedding of Alfred Daniel to Naomi Barber. Left to right: Christine, Naomi, Alfred Daniel, Martin Jr.

From left to right:
Martin Jr., Isaac
Farris Sr., Alfred
Daniel, and
Martin Sr.

Right: The wedding
of Christine King
to Isaac Newton
Farris Sr. in 1960
at Ebenezer Baptist
Church, Atlanta.
Alfred Daniel (left)
and Martin Jr.
(right) are both
officiating.

SHARING THOUGHTS, IDEAS, AND DREAMS within Martin Luther King Jr.'s family circle was an experience rich with understanding and compassion and true to the enrichment of family bonding. Feeling the warmth and wisdom of his presence in family fellowship enhanced the spirit of my own life. I remember when I first met him, he and Coretta were staying at the home of his parents, Rev. and Mrs. Martin Luther King Sr., where their daughter, my fiancé, Christine, also lived. I met him one evening when I came to visit Christine. She introduced him as "ML," so that's what I always called him, just as others who were close to him did. He shook my hand, and we sat down. We sat and talked together with Coretta and Christine in the living room of the home. ML had on a house robe, as he had been resting. We talked very generally, getting to know one another. It was quite a comfortable conversation.

After Christine and I married, shortly after we moved into our first home, ML wanted to give us something for the house. He gave us a very wonderful gift, a dining room set, complete with a table, chairs, china cabinet, and buffet table. No doubt it was a gift from his heart, and Christine and I greatly appreciated it.

My heart always beats with excitement and enthusiasm when I witness examples of his strength to love and his fight for justice and equality. Martin Luther King Jr.'s leadership inspired people from all walks of life to believe in themselves, to strive to achieve something, to work harder, to give more, to reach for brotherhood, to love one another, to search for truth, and to believe in the kindred spirit of all mankind.

He changed many lives in his quest for justice. His nonviolent way of encountering the challenges of life added a powerful dimension to how we live and relate and communicate. When we study that leadership, we become acutely aware of the courageous love that he promoted.

Thank you, God, for your gift of Martin Luther King Jr. He came before us at a time when the flames of hope were flickering away. In the end, he gave his life, but the seeds of hope had been planted in the hearts of many people throughout the world. The inspiration his life gave us echoed across the span of the earth, and the hope for freedom and justice blossomed fervently.

As a member of the Alpha Phi Alpha fraternity, I am both thankful and proud of the work inspired and led by this organization in the development of the special memorial in Washington, DC, commemorating the life of Martin Luther King Jr. I am also deeply grateful for the contributions of many individuals and organizations that supported the project financially.

Situated in the shadows of the Lincoln Memorial and the nation's capitol, it fills us with the remembrance of King's melodious voice and inspiring words as he told the world of his dream. Now the dream lives on. When we embrace the full meaning of this monument of hope and this symbol of peace, this beacon of courage will be a source of inspiration for many ages to come.

Martin Luther King Jr. marched into our lives and created a whole new melody of meaning and purpose. I bask in the sunshine of hope inspired by his life. When I read his words, I find comfort and reassurance. As I encounter the challenges of living, I find strength in his wisdom, and my soul is restored.

Somehow, I know that unborn generations will find inspiration, refuge, and peace in the glory of his presence that is represented by this powerful monument.

May God continue to bless all of us as we journey toward the promised land.

ISAAC N. FARRIS SR.
Brother-in-law

KING FAMILY
BRANCHES

**ALVEDA C. KING, DEREK B. KING,
ISAAC NEWTON FARRIS JR.,
ANGELA FARRIS WATKINS**
Nieces and Nephews

Christmas 1961 at the Johnson Avenue, Atlanta, home of Martin Jr. and Coretta. From left to right, bottom row: Yolanda Denise King, Martin III, Darlene King. Middle row: Alfred Daniel II, Martin Sr. holding Vernon Christopher King, Alberta Williams King holding Dexter Scott King, Derek Barber King. Top row (standing): Alfred Daniel, Naomi Barber King, Isaac N. Farris Sr., Christine, Alveda King, Coretta, Martin Jr.

The twenty-fifth wedding
anniversary of Martin Luther
King Sr. and Alberta Williams
King, at their Boulevard home
in Northeast Atlanta. From left
to right (standing): Christine,
Martin Jr., Alberta Williams
King, Alveda King (daughter
of Naomi and Alfred Daniel),
Naomi Barber King, Alfred
Daniel. Seated: Martin Sr.

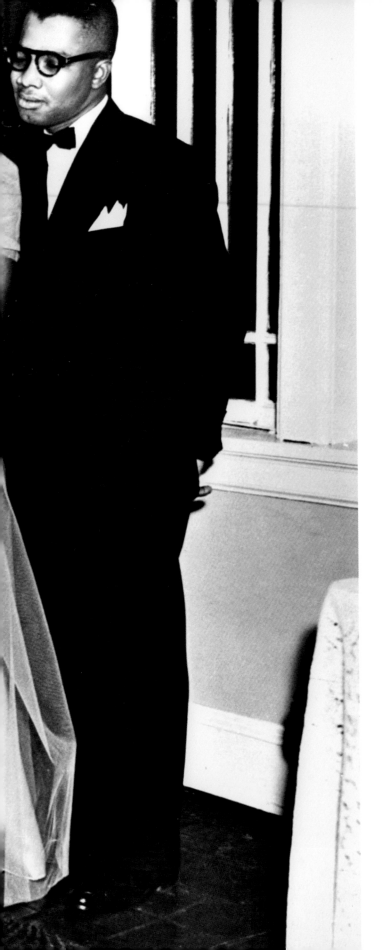

After the marriages of Martin Jr., Alfred Daniel, and Christine, children were born, making up the next generation of the King family.

AS ONE OF THE AUTHORS of the Martin Luther King Jr. holiday legislation, I was standing tall on the day Uncle ML's portrait was hung in the halls of the Georgia State Capitol. I remember wondering if I could ever walk a mile in his shoes.

Speaking of shoes, I remember a special moment during a family gathering at the home where Uncle ML, Aunt Coretta, and their children lived in Atlanta. I was a curious teenager who wanted to know more about this man who was always in the news. So I decided to follow him around the house. I tried not to be too obvious, but I suspect he was onto my little game from the start. When he excused himself for a moment to go to his "study" (an old-fashioned word for home office), I slipped out behind him to peek around the doorway. He sat down, stretched his arms above his head, and sighed. He reached down to untie his shoes. I tiptoed in to give him his house shoes. (The women in our family always kept house slippers close for the men. It was a family tradition.) Uncle ML stepped into the shoes. His smile was as bright as sunshine. His voice was deep yet gentle. "Ah, Alveda," he chuckled. "You're such a pretty girl. And you're growing up. We're going have to chase the boys away one day." That assurance, that he was looking out for me, just like my daddy and granddaddy did, was so comforting. It was always like that in his presence. He made me feel so safe, and so loved.

It was this same love that inspired the King Center, the only living memorial to my uncle, located in Atlanta, Georgia. The whole family worked with Aunt Coretta to help establish the memorial to her husband. I was coeditor of the King Center newsletter and Aunt Coretta's personal assistant and traveling companion; I worked with Yolanda in her role as director of the cultural affairs program.

During those days, I wrote the song "Let Freedom Ring, and Thank God That King Had a Dream." Uncle ML's dream was rooted not only in the "American Dream"—it was firmly established in the love of God.

This same love inspires my children and grandchildren today. My son John often reflects on his destiny as he gazes at the portrait of Uncle ML hanging high on the wall in his room. My son Jarrett's published commentaries inspired by his great-uncle ML, granddaddy AD, and great-granddaddy King are making a mark for justice and righteousness. I remember the day that my son Eddie said that he wanted to protect society's weakest, the unborn. I enjoy the many discussions with my son Joshua regarding his uncle ML's philosophical writings. There are precious moments with my daughters, Celeste and Jennifer, when they join me in sharing the platform of life, liberty, and freedom for all, from conception until natural death. The joy of seeing my children, their spouses, and the grandchildren embrace Uncle ML's dream is remarkable.

Today as a mother, grandmother, and ordained minister of the Gospel of Jesus Christ, I know that my uncle was right, that love for God, for family, and for all of humanity is the key to solving the problems of the world. This love inspired the gift of the King Center in Atlanta, and now the National King Memorial in Washington, DC. May God's love inspire us all to remember my dear uncle ML.

ALVEDA C. KING

Niece

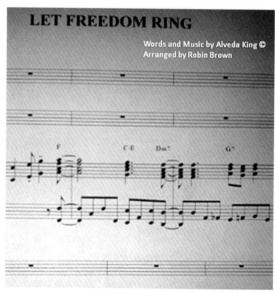

Top: Alveda King, then a Georgia State Representative, stands in front of a portrait of her uncle Martin Luther King Jr. at the Georgia State Capitol.

Bottom: "Let Freedom Ring," a song written by Alveda King in memory of her late uncle and his famous "I Have a Dream Speech."

Descendants of Martin Luther King Jr. The children and grandchildren of Martin Jr.'s niece Alveda King on the steps of the house in Atlanta where Martin Jr. was born and lived as a child. Pictured on the left side of the stairs: Jaden Ellis, Daniel Ellis, and Alveda King holding one of her granddaughters, Maryn Rippy. Pictured on the right side of the stairs: Aaron Ellis, Gabriel Ellis. Pictured on the back row, left to right: Uriah Ellis, Eddie Beal III, Ebonie Beal, John Beal, Jennifer Beal, Joshua Beal, Celeste Beal McFadgen, Annetta Ellis, Lonice McFadgen, Jarrett Ellis. Seated: Naomi Barber King holding one of her great grandsons, Steven McFadgen II.

"There is a sense of pride when I think about the fact that a guy I share DNA with, a guy who precedes me by only one generation, and a guy I actually knew has a monument in his honor in the A-list section on the Mall in the nation's capital."

UNFORTUNATELY, I never met Rev. Dr. Martin Luther King Jr., but fortunately, I did meet Uncle ML. During his lifetime, I was too young to understand or be aware of the societal injustices that were surrounding me—and certainly too young to comprehend his great dream for America or his nonviolent philosophy as an instruction manual on how to live one's life. The man I met was Uncle ML (short for Martin Luther), the name he was referred to by his parents, siblings, family, and friends as he was growing up to become Dr. King. My memories are of a guy I used to play with at my house. When he would come for a visit, we would often play hide-and-seek. It was such fun. I also remember him coming for our annual Thanksgiving dinner, at our home, and he would slip away to another room to get a quick nap. It would be years before I could appreciate how the mantle of leadership, the weight of his work, and travel schedule created conditions where he desperately needed those quick naps. I do have a very vague memory or two of him in the pulpit of Ebenezer Baptist, our family church, but my memories are overwhelmingly of a playful, comical man. Just as in his work as a man of the cloth and as a human and civil rights leader, Uncle ML, during his family and friend time, was determined to bring joy, relief, and laughter to those surrounding him. Aside from remembering

playing with him, I vividly remember the fun effect he had on others. After his assassination, as I grew and learned of his work, I recognized in his work the compassion I saw at home.

As I grew to comprehend his philosophy and meet "Dr. King," I realized that one of the true regrets that I will have in life is that I was not old enough for us to have worked together as we played together. I can only imagine the multitude of citizens, both black and white, both male and female, the old and the young, whose names are not held up in the bright lights but who enabled him to be the great Dr. King. I can only imagine how they must feel having been a part of a revolution that not only changed our country, but the world.

There is a sense of pride when I think about the fact that a guy I share DNA with, a guy who precedes me by only one generation, and a guy I actually knew has a monument in his honor in the A-list section on the Mall in the nation's capital. I know my fellow African Americans have a sense of pride knowing that a person that looks like them has a place alongside some of our greatest presidents. But for me the proudest thing—and I think it would be the proudest thing for Uncle ML—is the long-term impact this will have on American society. In the immediate term, the focus will probably center on the fact that this is the first monument to an African American, but long term, the more important first will

The King family at Christmas at the home of Rev. and Mrs. Martin Luther King Sr. in Atlanta, Georgia. Seated left to right, bottom row: Alfred Daniel Williams King II, Yolanda Denise King, Martin Luther King III, Alberta Williams King holding Vernon Christopher King, Alveda King holding Isaac Newton Farris Jr., Martin Sr. holding Dexter Scott King, Darlene King, Derek Barber King. Left to right, top row: Martin Jr., Coretta Scott King, Christine King Farris, Isaac N. Farris Sr., Naomi Barber King, Alfred Daniel Williams King.

be recognized and appreciated. The more important first and the true point of pride for me is this monument will be the first monument to PEACE and NONVIOLENCE on the Mall. This in no way is a criticism or negative reflection on the other existing monuments; they all deserve to be there, just like the monument to Uncle ML. But the monument to Uncle ML will provide for future generations an example of a citizen leader who led, fought, and won a war without ever having fired a shot.

Future generations will see an army of black and white, male and female, old and young that met the violence of attack dogs, billy clubs, water hoses, bombings, gunfire, and lynchings with the nonviolence of passive resistance, and peace and love for one's fellow human being. Future generations will know it is possible to meet violence with nonviolence and win. They will know that conflicts can be resolved without use of weapons, that rights don't have to be achieved at the point of a gun. This monument will be a gathering place for people of all hues, any ethnicity and any religious orientation, or no religious orientation, to gather to nonviolently protest for rights. This monument will be both a reminder and example to people around the world of how they can change the negative aspects of their societies while preserving the best and, most important, preserving life and the infrastructure needed to maintain it. Similarly, the

national holiday commemorating Uncle ML's life has become much more than a day of hero worship of one man—millions of Americans dedicate the day to performing acts of service to others. In fact, it's the only holiday on the American calendar whose official designation states that it is not a day for play but a day of service to others. Because of what Uncle ML did as a citizen leader, the principles he fought and stood for, this monument will follow that tradition and become not just a memorial to the man but an inspirational NONVIOLENT path to a more caring, a more peaceful, and a more just society. As one who shares DNA with a guy who I personally consider the greatest leader of the twentieth century, its not the brick and mortar on the Mall that gives me the greatest sense of pride but the lesson that it conveys: CHANGE THROUGH NONVIOLENCE. Congratulations, Uncle ML, on a life well lived.

ISAAC NEWTON FARRIS JR.
Nephew

Martin Luther King Jr. holding his niece Angela Farris.

Angela Farris Watkins in front of the statue of her uncle at the Martin Luther King Jr. National Memorial in Washington, DC.

I **WAS VERY YOUNG** when I knew my dear uncle ML (as we affectionately called him), but the delight that I felt when he was around glows as brightly today as it did back then. I remember the times I saw him. He was always very playful, and I remember him as somewhat of an adult playmate for me. His smile and laughter were very amusing. I remember seeing him in our church, Ebenezer Baptist Church, on Sunday morning after worship service and how he would pick me up and give me a kiss and a hug. I have seen the telegram he sent to my mother, his sister, when I was born, congratulating her on my birth and welcoming me to the world. When I look at the pictures of him holding me and playing with me, I remember what it was like seeing him and being comforted by his joy.

As an adult, I know him to be even more special than I thought he was then. He was as normal as he was odd. He was a regular guy—a family man, a scholar, and a preacher—and yet he was odd to the degree that he made the ultimate commitment to America. With his faith, his scholarship, and his heart of love, he faced the ugliness and horror of injustice with an abiding love for all humanity. I know now that he was the greatest teacher for all of us. He had an unusual gift of showing and sharing love, despite the challenges and the hatred and bitterness around him.

A few years ago, as I was writing a supplemental psychology text, I discovered him again. I found his speech to a body of psychologists at the American Psychological Association convention and, suddenly, it dawned on me that Uncle ML was a psychologist himself; he was speaking, writing, and preaching to America about exhibiting our "best behavior," both individually and collectively—through nonviolent resistance to evil, brotherhood, the beloved community, equality, justice, and freedom. He taught us how to guard and guide our thoughts about one another so that we might serve one another.

I am remembering his fondness for me, as well as his commitment to America, in the children's books I write, to make sure that generations of children understand what he did. I am remembering him in the college courses that I teach, to make sure that budding young psychologists understand his school of thought and his winning principles. I am remembering him in the Kingian Nonviolence trainings that I conduct with students, schoolteachers, and corporate executives who yearn for his ethical model of leadership.

I am so proud to call him my uncle, for all that he was to so many people. I see him now, as I did when I was young, standing really, really tall. I salute my uncle ML for his endurance, his strength, his commitment, his unselfishness, for serving God and man, and for always showing and sharing his love. I love you, Uncle ML, and miss you dearly!

ANGELA FARRIS WATKINS, PHD
Niece

Martin Jr. in the shadow of his nephew Derek Barber King.

HAVE TWO behind-the-scenes recollections of my uncle ML. The first one happened in 1965 or 1966 at our home in Louisville, Kentucky. My father, Rev. AD King Sr., was the president of the Kentucky Christian Leadership Conference (KCLC), and at that time, KCLC was immersed in a housing campaign. Uncle ML came to town to give the project a boost. He stopped by the house to greet everybody. He and Daddy ended up in Daddy and Mama's room, wrestling on the bed like two children! It should be noted that these were men in their thirties.

The second recollection took place on Thanksgiving Day in Atlanta in 1967, when our family gathered at the home of Uncle ML and Aunt Coretta. I had the nerve to challenge Uncle ML to a game of eight ball on his pool table. He let me break, and I sank one ball on the break. I took my next shot and missed. Uncle ML ran the table on me. After the game, he laughed and gave me a pat on the head and said to keep practicing—I would get good.

I cite these two occurrences to point out that Martin Luther King was not some larger-than-life icon who had no personal or family life. To the contrary, he was and is still Uncle ML.

There is one other experience I would like to note. After Uncle ML and Daddy died, I knew I had a call to serve. So I went to Morehouse College as they did. I studied under instructors who had taught them. I went to seminary in Rochester, New York, and studied under some of the instructors who taught Uncle ML. Coincidence? I think not. I now fully ascribe to and practice the principles of nonviolence that Uncle ML advocated. I look at him as a mentor. I have listened to speeches and sermons that he delivered; I have read books and articles he wrote, and they had a tremendous impact on me, to the point that I am following the path he walked. As he believed in the potential of good and civility in the human spirit, so do I. With every ounce of essence in my being, I too believe that we will overcome.

DEREK B. KING

Nephew

A PROTÉGÉ OF MARTIN LUTHER KING JR.

ALBERT PAUL BRINSON
Ebenezer Baptist Church

Martin Luther King Jr., Albert Paul Brinson, and Alfred Daniel Williams King

Among the many things Martin Luther King Jr. accomplished, he was also a mentor. He always had time to advise young men who were following his lead. Many of them were inspired, as he was, to join the ministry.

PERSONAL MEMORIES OF Dr. Martin Luther King Jr. rise high in my mental sky:

- Ebenezer Baptist Church in Atlanta, Georgia, the home of Rev. Martin Luther King Sr. and Mrs. Alberta Williams King and their children, Christine, "ML," and "AD," are living monuments in my life, the life of a little Negro boy growing up in the segregated South in the 1940s.

- In 1955, when "ML" had become Dr. Martin Luther King Jr., pastor of Dexter Avenue Baptist Church and the chosen leader of the Montgomery, Alabama, bus boycott, I was a senior at David T. Howard High School in Atlanta, swept up in the hopes of those times, strongly inspired by what was occurring.

- My first hands-on-the-wheel highway driving experience was with Rev. King Sr. from Atlanta to Montgomery to the home of Martin and Coretta King.

- In January of 1960, Dr. King Jr. accepted the invitation from our home church, Ebenezer, to become the church's first copastor, along with his father, and to expand the outreach of the growing Civil Rights Movement.

- In March of 1960, as a senior at Morehouse College, I became one of the organizers of Atlanta's student sit-in movement, the Committee on Appeal for Human Rights, which ultimately resulted in the desegregation of lunch counters and restaurants in the city.

In the spring of 1963, as an Atlanta Public Schools colored teacher, I found myself in Birmingham, Alabama, with Rev. King Sr. during Holy Week, leading up to Easter Sunday. This was the time of the water hoses and dogs, which were used to turn back the protestors marching against segregation. It was an experience I will never forget, a life-changing experience. I knew that there was something pulling on me. It had been for quite some time. And I knew what it was. It was what I had heard about almost all of the time, the "call" to ministry. I was hearing God calling me to the Christian ministry.

I was literally terrified. I did not want to be a "preacher." I certainly did not see myself as a person who was good enough to fill such a role and lifestyle. My wife of three years had not married a minister. It was clear to me that I did not know what to do with my overpowering feelings.

One evening in May, without speaking to anyone else, I finally got the courage to go over to the Johnson Avenue home of ML and Coretta. She was there with the kids along with Cody Perry, who was a driver and aide to Dr. King Jr. and the family. I told her that I needed to talk with ML about something very important. She immediately responded by letting me know that it was good that I had come by, because Cody needed to leave and would not return until early in the morning. She asked if I could meet Martin at the Atlanta Airport in his stead. It was already after five, and his plane would arrive about six forty-five.

ML was a little surprised when I was there instead of Cody, but he was glad to see me anyway. After walking to the car in the midst of a lot of people, we rode through some construction work, through downtown Atlanta, and into Atlanta's Fourth Ward district.

After some conversation about his trip, I told him that I had something very important to talk with him about, not really knowing how to begin the conversation.

Without hesitation, he interrupted me with a smile, saying, "I know what you want to talk about. It's no surprise to me. . . . You are dealing with your call to ministry."

We began a conversation that lasted until after midnight. I told him of how frightened and unworthy I felt to even approach the conversation about me as a preacher or minister. I felt that I wasn't good enough. He looked at me and spoke about himself, assuring me that "we are never good enough." He said God uses us in spite of ourselves, never because we are worthy.

I was still in a state of shock, but we talked about what I would do. The first thing was to resign my teaching position at the end of the semester. He would talk to Dr. Harry Richardson, president of the Interdenominational Theological Center, so I could begin my seminary education in September. He took out his date book and suggested Sunday, August 4, when I would preach my initial sermon. He did not believe in a "trial" sermon. He reminded me that I was not on trial. I think I finally brought up a smile. I would begin learning ministry firsthand by assisting him and Daddy King.

On that Sunday morning, August 4, 1963, Dr. Martin Luther King Jr. preached for the morning worship and urged the membership to be present at the evening communion service, where Albert Paul Brinson, who grew up in this church, would preach his first sermon and be licensed to the Christian ministry.

That evening, having resigned my teaching job, enrolled in seminary, and prepared my sermon, we prayed together, Rev. King Jr. and me. Rev. King Sr. beamed with pride. ML looked at me and smiled. He said, "Albert, you look scared." He was so right.

I followed him and Rev. King Sr. out of the study into the archway bridge from the educational building of the church that led directly into the pulpit, assured and certain that I finally knew the purpose and calling of my life. I walked into a full church of Ebenezer members and well-wishers from the Atlanta community.

There would be many moments, times, and events that I shared with Martin Luther King Jr., but none more powerful than that evening in May of 1963 and the conversation that sent me forth in ministry, always remembering what he said, that God uses us not because of, but in spite of, ourselves.

ALBERT PAUL BRINSON
Ebenezer Baptist Church

THE COMING OF ANOTHER GENERATION

**FARRIS CHRISTINE WATKINS, JARRETT ELLIS, DEREK KING II,
KYLE KING, VICTORIA KING, VENUS KING**

Great-nephews and Great-nieces

And their children had children, who continued the legacy in their own right.

Dear Uncle ML,

I never had the chance or the privilege of meeting you, but my family has told me so many stories about you, that I feel like I do know you. It started with different people telling me how you changed their lives and made a difference for my generation and others unborn. Then it was my grandmother Christine King Farris and her book that let me know that not only were you a civil rights giant, you were a kid like me, who loved to play and joke around with your sister and brother! Next it was my mother, Angela Farris Watkins, who taught me the value of family through your love as a family man. Then, as I got older, I realized that you were not only a civil rights giant, or a kid that loved to play, or a family man, you were also a preacher. Through the voices of my church family at Ebenezer Baptist Church, I heard from many people how you took after your father and preached the good news and the Gospel of Jesus Christ. The church also told me that you implemented the Gospel into the movement, your speeches, and marches. In school, my teachers would teach me about you. As they went step by step, explaining to the other children in the class what you did to make a difference, I thought to myself, "Wow, a man like this couldn't have really come from my family," but sure enough, you did, and I thank God for you.

Every year, at the Martin Luther King Jr. Commemorative Service, in Atlanta, my peers and I recite a litany in commemoration of you. As I watch my peers, I see how they come to understand you more and realize just how important you are. So when we are on the pulpit saying the litany, we are saying what we really believe about you.

When I found out that a monument was going to be built for you on the Mall in Washington, DC, I wasn't surprised at all. Actually, I was trying to figure out why this hadn't been done before! But I soon realized that everything has a time and a place. Uncle ML, this is your time to be celebrated. Not just because of the difference you made in everybody's life, but because you died working and trying to save our country. Just like the people who fought and died for their country in World War II, Korea, and Vietnam, you deserve a monument, too. Not only do you deserve a monument because of this, but also because you are a child of God who did not say no when He was in your kitchen and told you what you were up against. You knew that God would be there for you through all of the turmoil and turbulence you would have to go through to achieve what you did. You knew that for your dream to come true, you would have to have help that was much bigger than any person on earth. Because of your faith, belief, and persistence, you deserve the honor, Uncle ML.

Your great-niece,
FARRIS CHRISTINE WATKINS

THOUGH I NEVER HAD the opportunity to meet my great-uncle Martin, who departed this life two years before my birth, I had the great privilege of getting to know him through those he was closest to in life. Great-granddaddy King Sr., Great-grandmother Alberta King, Aunt Coretta Scott King, and Aunt Christine King Farris all radiated the noble-heartedness and strength that typified the greatness of Uncle Martin and enabled him to set forth an example that changed the world. My grandmother, Naomi King, embodies this same grace and also helps me to connect with her husband and my grandfather, AD King, who worked so closely with Uncle ML as the "brother of the dreamer."

In my formative years, I received a legacy founded upon the principles of love and devotion to God and to family, most immediately to those bound by blood and vows, yes, but just as importantly, to the entire human community as far as the Lord may lead. This is the man I understood Uncle Martin to be from those who knew him best. This is the kind of man I was encouraged and expected to be by those who gave so freely of their lives to ensure that I could live mine well.

Today, I am trying to represent Uncle Martin's commitment and have tried to do so over the years. I went to Oral Roberts University and, like Great-granddaddy King, Uncle Martin, Granddaddy AD, and his sons Derek Sr. and Vernon, studied the Bible to understand the person and ministry of Christ, whose mission to deliver the Gospel of Grace provided the example of, and inspiration for, the King family's continuing mission to bring hope and reconciliation to a world in conflict.

While later earning a law degree, I developed a particular appreciation for the American system of jurisprudence, which allows citizens to fight for the rights that are due to each of us through our nation's charter. I understood the power of Uncle ML's strategy of nonviolence that brought forth justice, not by the strength of arms, but by the irresistible appeal to righteousness that called for those in power to do unto others as they would have done to them in their own lives. Uncle ML called on a nation that defined itself by an indomitable spirit of liberty to live up to its creed. From that charge came the Civil Rights Act of 1964, *Heart of Atlanta Motel v. United States,* and the Voting Rights Act of 1965. A generation after these monumental acts of legislation and judicial interpretation, I am able to practice law in a firm that is known as one of the largest and most diverse in the nation. I have had the privilege of helping to elect this country's first African American president. Most important, I am able to raise my children in a land where they are increasingly judged by the content of their character rather than by the color of their skin.

Uncle ML made a great contribution to our world, and so I am determined to do my part. Inspired by his life and the legacy of the King family received from my grandfather AD King and reinforced by all of the King family members who raised me, I will work for righteousness and justice in the spirit of God's love to hopefully make the world a better place not only for my wife, sons, siblings, descendants of AD King, Christine King Farris, and Martin Luther King Jr., but for all humanity as far as the Lord may lead.

JARRETT ELLIS
Great-nephew

EVEN THOUGH we never met face to face, through our daddy's teachings that he got from you, our granddaddy Rev. AD Williams Sr., and our great-granddaddy Rev. Martin Luther King Sr., we feel that we have met you, and we must keep the dream alive by doing the will of God. We don't have our daddy, Rev. Vernon C. King, with us because he died on Friday, May 1, 2009. And America doesn't have you, but we still know what is expected. We know that we must follow the teachings of Jesus Christ as you and our father did. We know we must follow the six principles of nonviolence as you taught America. Yes, Uncle Martin, you have left so much for us to do, and we can and will. Our mother, Robin Scott King, tells us that we must be the best because we are the ones who will have to make our world a better place to live.

Therefore, we cherish the memories that our father shared with us about you, how you gave your life for the common citizen, and how you were the chosen one to move people to another level of freedom that was denied African Americans. We are so blessed and really don't know what it was like to be denied the right to sit in the front of the bus or drink from the same water fountain as white people or not be able to be friends with white people. So we say thank you, Uncle Martin, for standing up and not being scared to do the will of God to make our world a better place. We won't let you or our daddy down; we will remember the difference you made because, as our mom teaches us, we are the best, no weapon formed against us shall prosper, and the best is yet to come.

Your great-nieces, Victoria and Venus King, know you gave your best, showed your best, and were the chosen best by God, and we can do so because you did! We even have proof from God's word in the book of Philippians 4:13: We can do all things through Christ Jesus, who strengthens us.

VICTORIA AND VENUS KING

Great-nieces

WE ARE Derek Barber King II and Kyle Nelson Wendell King, great-nephews of Uncle ML. We were not born during Uncle ML's lifetime. However, that does not mean that we are disconnected. Our father, Derek Barber King Sr., has taught us who Uncle ML is. In our limited travels, we have ridden on streets in various parts of the country that bear his name. We have seen movies depicting his life and work. His image is everywhere.

During family gatherings, we hear stories about the kind of man he was behind the scenes. He was a practical joker, funny, compassionate, and generous. He took out time to be with family. Like the Star Wars movie series talks about the "Force," Uncle ML is part of the Force, and the Force is with us and all around us.

DEREK II AND KYLE KING

Great-nephews

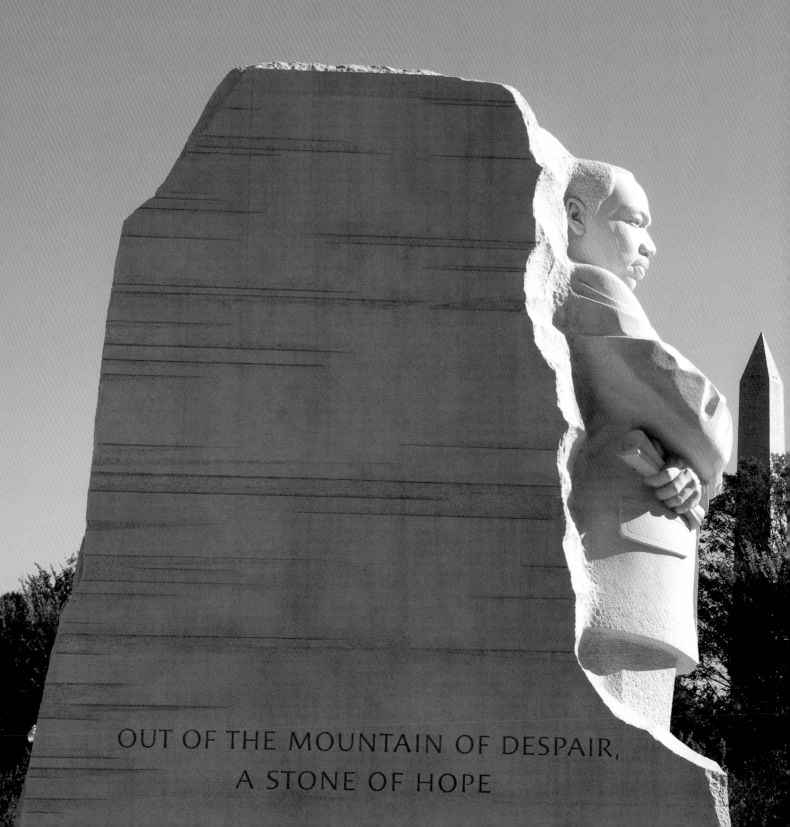

OUT OF THE MOUNTAIN OF DESPAIR,
A STONE OF HOPE

SALUTE FROM AMERICA: THE MARTIN LUTHER KING JR. NATIONAL MEMORIAL

The King family in front of Stone of Hope. Left to right: Angela Farris Watkins, Farris Christine Watkins, Isaac N. Farris Sr., Alveda King, Christine King Farris, Bernice A. King, Arndrea King (wife of Martin III), Martin Luther King III. In front is Yolanda Renee King, daughter of Mr. & Mrs. King III.

America too continues the legacy in its salute to Dr. King, building his memorial in a place of prominence and significance to the nation, as well as to his life and works.

HOW APPROPRIATE that Martin Luther King Jr. would be honored with a memorial on the National Mall in Washington, DC, reserved until now for presidents of the United States. It was the idea of Martin Luther King Jr.'s fraternity, Alpha Phi Alpha. With stellar leadership, they organized a team of architects, designers, builders, philanthropists, and staff, and spent years working to persuade the United States Congress to appropriately honor a man who left our nation and our world much better than he found it.

Yet Martin Luther King Jr. would never have expected or wanted such an honor. As he said in what would be one of his final speeches, he wanted only to be remembered as a drum major for justice and a drum major for peace. He wanted to live a committed life, helping somebody as he passed along. He did much more than that.

As you witness and reflect upon this great memorial, may you see this King of Heart and feel the power and the love that he expressed.

Top: *Entering the King memorial from the Inscription Wall.*

Bottom: *The King family at the statue of Martin Luther King Jr.,* Stone of Hope, *before the opening of the King memorial. Left to right: Alveda King, Naomi Barber King, Christine King Farris, Bernice A. King, Isaac Farris Jr., Farris Christine Watkins, Isaac Farris Sr., Angela Farris Watkins.*

*Night view, the
Inscription Wall at
the King memorial.*

*Opposite: Front
view, statue of
Martin Luther King
Jr.,* Stone of Hope.

Close View, Martin Luther King Jr.'s sister, Christine King Farris, elevated to eye level of the statue Stone of Hope.

Opposite: Angle view, statue of Martin Luther King Jr., Stone of Hope.

AFTERWORD

BEATITUDES

(Inspired by biblical text on the twentieth anniversary of Martin Luther King's "I Have A Dream" speech)

1. BLESSED are those who lack any negative spirit of the world—any spirit of worldliness—for their life is in THE KINGDOM OF GOD.

2. BLESSED are those who mourn because they are hurt by the spirit of evil in the world, for they shall be comforted in the bosom of THE SPIRIT OF GOD.

3. BLESSED are GOD'S gentle, human souls, for in their gentle, persistent patience in GOD, they will reap harvests of GOD'S SPIRITUAL INHERITANCE on and in the earth.

4. BLESSED are those who ache with pains of hunger for THE TRUTH OF GOD, whose spiritual throats are parched from consistent thirst for the TRUTH OF GOD and THE RIGHTEOUSNESS OF GOD, for their souls will be overshadowed, refilled to overflow, so that they are born anew in GOD.

5. BLESSED are those who live in THE MERCY OF GOD, for throughout their living, they shall reap harvests of plenty in the renewed and renewing MERCY OF GOD.

6. BLESSED are those who are pure in heart, for purity in THE SPIRIT OF GOD, through CHRIST, is the prerequisite for the vision to see GOD.

7. BLESSED are those whose living does not compromise or confound THE TRUTH OF GOD that brings THE PEACE OF GOD to those worn by the sin-filled rebellion of the world, for by their loving hearts, they shall be called the CHILDREN OF GOD.

8. BLESSED are those whose daily living is dedicated to GOD in and for GOD'S RIGHTEOUSNESS, to the extent that they allow their lives to be persecuted on account of their dedication to THE RIGHTEOUSNESS OF GOD, for their inheritance is THE KINGDOM OF GOD.

9. BLESSED are those who are ridiculed, rejected, unsung, ignored, overlooked, understated, oppressed, reviled, and persecuted falsely for THE SAKE OF GOD, through CHRIST, for great in HEAVEN is their reward, and great is their joy in HEAVEN.

AMEN.

DR. CAREY WYNN II
August 1983

CONTRIBUTORS

REV. DR. MARTIN LUTHER KING SR.

(Father of Martin Luther King Jr.)

Posthumous contributor. Dr. King Sr. (1899–1984) was the third pastor in the history of Ebenezer Baptist Church, in Atlanta, Georgia. He was the husband of Alberta Christine Williams King and the father of three children, Christine, Martin Jr., and Alfred Daniel. As a noted advocate for social justice, he led the successful campaign to equalize African American teachers' salaries with those of white teachers. He was also instrumental in leading voter registration drives at his church. Dr. King Sr. retired as the pastor of Ebenezer in 1975.

MRS. ALBERTA CHRISTINE WILLIAMS KING

(Mother of Martin Luther King Jr.)

Posthumous contributor. Mrs. Alberta King (1903–1974) was a wonderful and cherished wife and mother. She served as church organist, choir director, and women's ministry leader at Ebenezer Baptist Church, in Atlanta, for many, many years. She loved to tell jokes and meet new people. She was genuinely a nurturer and builder of a great legacy.

DR. CHRISTINE KING FARRIS

(Sister of Martin Luther King Jr.)

Willie Christine King was born to Rev. Martin Luther King Sr. and Alberta Williams King on September 11, 1927. Christine was a role model for her younger brothers, Martin Jr. and Alfred Daniel. Her decision to step forward during a church revival meeting became the stimulus for a decisive moment in Martin Jr.'s religious life. As he later wrote, "My sister was the first one to join the church that morning and after seeing her join I decided that I would not let her get ahead of me, so I was the next."

Christine also excelled academically. She attended public and private schools in Atlanta: Younge Street Elementary School, Atlanta University's Oglethorpe Elementary and Laboratory High Schools, and Booker T. Washington High School. She received a bachelor of arts degree in economics from Spelman College in 1948. She obtained a master of arts degree in the social foundations of education in 1950 and, in 1958, a master of arts in special education at Columbia University's Teachers College.

Christine began her teaching career at W. H. Crogman Elementary School in the Atlanta Public Schools. She went on to work as an adjunct professor at Morehouse College and Atlanta University and as an associate professor of education at Spelman College.

In December of 1955, when Martin Jr. was elected president of the Montgomery Improvement Association and designated spokesman for the Montgomery boycott, her entire family was swept up in one of America's most exciting and meaningful historical movements. Christine took an active part in nonviolent demonstrations, including the historic Selma-to-Montgomery March for voting rights in 1965 and the March Against Fear in Mississippi in 1966.

On August 19, 1960, Christine married Isaac Newton Farris, and that marriage produced two children, Isaac Jr. and Angela. Christine also has one grandchild, Farris, daughter of Angela.

When Martin Jr. was assassinated in April 1968, Christine resolved that she would play an active role in efforts to ensure that her brother's life and teachings would not be forgotten. She joined with her sister-in-law Coretta in planning for what became the Martin Luther King Jr. National Historic Site and Preservation District—the preservation of her family's birth home, Ebenezer Baptist Church, her brother's permanent entombment, and the Martin Luther King Jr. Center for Nonviolent Social Change—now a place of pilgrimage attracting people from all over the world. She serves today as the King Center's vice chair and treasurer.

In addition to her instrumental role in securing her brother's legacy, Christine King Farris has built a distinguished career in her own right as an educator. Today she serves as director of the Spelman College Learning Resources Center, as well as an associate professor of education. She is the author of *My Brother Martin* and *March On*, both books for young readers; *Martin Luther King: His Life and Dream*, a text for educators; and *Through It All*, her personal memoir.

The recipient of more than a dozen major honors and awards, including the NAACP Image Award and the SCLC Septima Clark Award, Christine King Farris continues to dedicate her life to educating young people, promoting literacy, and advocating her brother's philosophy and strategy of nonviolence. For her contributions to the field of education, she was awarded an honorary doctorate from Bennett College in the spring of 2007.

Christine is a devoted member of Ebenezer Baptist Church, where she is the founder of the Christine King Farris Handbell Choirs and a coordinator of academic scholarships, as well as a member of the finance committee, church life and program committee, September Club, and trustee board. Christine is also a member of the Links, Inc., and Alpha Kappa Alpha Sorority. Little known to most, Christine is a humorous and creative lady, who loves to read, shop, and spend time with family and friends. Christine King Farris is a wonderful and precious gift from God. Through it all, she is still standing, still serving, and still moving.

REV. ALFRED DANIEL WILLIAMS KING
(Brother of Martin Luther King Jr.)

Posthumous contributor. Rev. Alfred Daniel (AD) Williams King (1930–1969) was born as the third and last child to Martin Luther King Sr. and Alberta Williams King. A graduate of Morehouse College, in Atlanta, AD King was noted as an advocate and minister of social justice. He partnered with Martin Jr. as his brother led the American Civil Rights Movement. AD King served as pastor of several church congregations, Mount Vernon First Baptist Church, in Newnan, Georgia; First Street Baptist Church in Ensley, Alabama; Zion Baptist Church in Louisville, Kentucky; and finally as copastor with his father at Ebenezer Baptist Church, in Atlanta. Like his brother, AD King experienced the brutalities of violence when his own house was bombed, and he also espoused the method of love and nonviolence. He was a leader of the Poor People's Campaign, a great husband, and the father of five children (Alveda, Alfred II, Derek, Darlene, and Vernon).

DR. SAMUEL DUBOIS COOK
(College classmate of Martin Luther King Jr.)

Dr. Samuel DuBois Cook is a retired Dillard University president and the first African American professor at Duke University. He taught political science at Southern University in Baton Rouge, Louisiana, in 1955. He moved to Atlanta University to begin teaching there in 1956 and became politically active. He worked on black voter registration and served as youth director of the NAACP of Georgia. Dr. Cook also taught at other colleges and universities, including the University of Illinois, University of California—Los Angeles, and Duke University. Dr. Cook served as president of Dillard University for twenty-two years. He is now retired but still lectures at universities and colleges around the country. He lives in Atlanta with his wife, Sylvia. They have two children and two grandchildren (twins).

MRS. NAOMI BARBER KING
(Sister-in-law of Martin Luther King Jr.)

Mrs. Naomi Ruth Barber King is the widow of the late Rev. Alfred Daniel Williams King and a civil rights advocate. Mrs. King is a beloved mother, grandmother, great-grandmother, relative, and friend, and a comfort and bright light to those in the church and communities she serves. Naomi is the inspiration of the documentary project *AD King: Brother to the Dreamer*. She is an author and public speaker who addresses important issues of the day.

ISAAC N. FARRIS SR.

(Brother-in-law of Martin Luther King Jr.)

Isaac N. Farris Sr. was born in Eolia, Missouri, to Cornelius and Blanche Farris. He graduated from Lincoln University (Missouri) and later moved to Atlanta, where he worked for many years as a linotypist for a local newspaper, the *Atlanta Daily World,* and also served in the United States Army. He met and married Christine King and worked with her and other members of the King family to build the Martin Luther King Jr. Center for Nonviolent Social Change, the only living memorial to Dr. King. He is the proprietor of Farris Color Visions. He and Christine have two children, Isaac Jr. and Angela, and one grandchild, Farris Christine.

DR. ALVEDA KING

(Niece of Martin Luther King Jr.)

Dr. Alveda Celeste King is the daughter of the late Rev. Alfred Daniel Williams King and his beloved wife, Naomi Barber King. She is the eldest of five children born to this family. Alveda is a minister and civil rights leader, who speaks out on behalf of human rights from conception until natural death. Alveda believes that unconditional love is the key to positive action. The "blessed mother of six living children and a blessed grandmother," Alveda is humbled to add to her list of positive life experiences film and music production, a past career of nineteen years as a college professor, two terms as a Georgia State Legislator, a presidential appointment, and authorship of several books and songs. She is the founder of King for America and director of African American Outreach for Priests for Life.

ISAAC NEWTON FARRIS JR.

(Nephew of Martin Luther King Jr.)

Isaac Newton Farris Jr. was born in Atlanta, Georgia, and attended his uncle's alma mater, Morehouse College where he majored in political science.

In 1984, Mr. Farris got his first hands-on experience as a political operative when he served as Georgia field coordinator for the Walter Mondale presidential campaign. A year later, he served as deputy manager for the reelection of Andrew Young as mayor of Atlanta. In 1986, he was campaign manager for Martin Luther King III in his successful bid to become a Fulton County Commissioner. From 1987 to 1992, he served in executive-level positions in government, where he was responsible for implementing policy.

Between 1992 and 1996, Mr. Farris was president and CEO of the Clean Air Industries Inc., a company that was not only involved in environmental cleanup but also developed a patent technology that allowed combustion engines of truck, buses, and cars to run on clean-burning natural (methane) gas.

In 1996, Mr. Farris was appointed chief operating officer of the Martin Luther King Jr. Center, and in 2005, he was appointed president and CEO of the King Center and served in that capacity until March 2010. In 2011, he was elected national president of the Southern Christian Leadership Conference.

ANGELA FARRIS WATKINS, PHD
(Niece of Martin Luther King Jr.)

Dr. Angela Farris Watkins is an educator, author, lecturer, and civil rights advocate. She earned a bachelor of arts degree (with honors) in child development from Spelman College and both a master's degree in early childhood education and a doctor of philosophy degree in educational psychology from Georgia State University. She is currently an associate professor of psychology at Spelman College and formerly served on the faculty of Morehouse College and Georgia State University, and taught in the Atlanta Public Schools system.

A longtime advocate against the injustices facing African American students, Dr. Farris Watkins is committed to culture-specific teaching methodologies and the needs of diverse students. She is also an expert in African American psychology and is the author of *African American Psychology Review*.

Dr. Farris Watkins has developed a model curriculum on HIV/AIDS prevention to call attention to the need for prevention programs targeted at African American college students and to challenge historically black colleges and universities to become involved in curricular initiatives as a way of fighting the epidemic. She has received several grants to support this effort from the United Negro College Fund, the American Psychological Association, and the National Institutes of Health, among others.

Trained in the philosophy of nonviolence espoused by Martin Luther King Jr., Dr. Farris Watkins conducts Kingian Nonviolence trainings to ensure that the history and principles of her uncle will be continually embraced. Dr. Farris Watkins has written two children's books about Dr. King, *My Uncle Martin's Big Heart* and *My Uncle Martin's Words for America*, and has a third book forthcoming, *Love Will See You Through*.

Dr. Farris Watkins is the daughter of Isaac and Christine (King) Farris and the mother of Farris Christine. She has one brother, Mr. Isaac N. Farris Jr.

REV. DEREK BARBER KING SR.

(Nephew of Martin Luther King Jr.)

Derek Barber King is the son of Rev. Alfred Daniel Williams King and Naomi Barber King. Derek graduated from Morehouse College in 1976, earning dual bachelor of arts degrees in religious studies and political theory. In 1979, he earned a master of divinity degree from Colgate Rochester Divinity School/Bexley Hall/Crozer Theological Seminary (a merger of three schools) in Rochester, New York. He has a doctor of divinity degree from Virginia Seminary and College in Lynchburg, Virginia, and Georgetown College in Lexington, Kentucky.

As a preacher, Dr. King is presently the assistant to the pastor of Ebenezer Missionary Baptist Church, located in Indianapolis, Indiana. Additionally, Dr. King organized the New Life Baptist Church of Christ in Rome, Georgia. He served as pastor of the Pleasant Grove Baptist Church in Rome, Georgia, and the Tabernacle Missionary Baptist Church in West Palm Beach, Florida. Dr. King also serves as a full-time professor of religious studies at Martin University in Indianapolis, Indiana. Prior to this appointment, he taught in college extension programs, denominational capacities, and public school systems.

REV. DR. ALBERT PAUL BRINSON

(Mentored by Martin Luther King Jr.)

Born in Atlanta, Georgia, Dr. Brinson completed his undergraduate education at Morehouse College. Postgraduate degrees include a master of divinity from the Interdenominational Theological Center, Atlanta, and a doctor of ministry from United Theological Seminary, Dayton, Ohio. He undertook other extensive study in programs at New York University and Boston University School of Theology.

Dr. Brinson was licensed to the Christian ministry by Dr. Martin Luther King Jr. in his home church, Ebenezer Baptist, in 1963 and ordained as an American Baptist minister by Drs. Martin Luther King Sr. and Jr. in 1964. He served as assistant minister to the copastors at Ebenezer for the next four years, then served as pastor for eleven years at Antioch Baptist Church, Corona, New York, and nine years at Bank Street Memorial Baptist Church, Norfolk, Virginia.

Dr. Brinson retired from the American Baptist Churches, USA, as Associate General Secretary. He served as a trainer for new ministers of missions support and leadership, the affirmative action office, staff to the American Baptist Churches general board denominational inclusiveness committee, a member of the staff advisory council to the American Baptist Churches biennial committee, and the president of the Valley Forge Ministers Council.

He is a member of Alpha Phi Alpha Fraternity, Inc. He has been married to the former Vivian Welch of Atlanta, Georgia, for fifty years. They have three children.

FARRIS CHRISTINE WATKINS

(Great-niece of Martin Luther King Jr.)

Farris Christine Watkins was born on January 22, 1997, to Willie A. Watkins and Angela Farris Watkins, PhD. She is a high school student and a graduate of Barbizon School of Modeling, both in Atlanta, Georgia. Farris is a high achiever, particularly in the areas of verbal skills and language. As a result of her academic performance, Farris was invited to be a member of Duke University's Talent Identification Program. Farris is also a gifted singer and orator. At her school, she has served as a soloist in the school honor chorus and she is now a member of the school's premier high school honor chorus.

At her church, Farris is a soloist and junior director in the youth choir. Her gift for singing has landed her several invitations at professional public gatherings. Among them are an Atlanta Hawks basketball game, where she sang the national anthem, and the Emmy Awards Lifetime Achievement Program in New York.

As a gifted orator, Farris is regularly asked to speak at youth programs, in churches, and around the community. Competing for the school debate team, she has brought home several team and individual awards. She is also a member of Jack and Jill of America, Inc. and a school varsity cheerleader.

JARRETT ELLIS

(Great-nephew of Martin Luther King Jr.)

Jarrett R. Ellis is an Atlanta-area attorney with experience in one of the top 100 largest law firms in the world. Formerly, he was an educator in the Georgia Public Schools system following a career in marketing with two leading public and private corporations. Jarrett lives in Mableton, Georgia, with his wife and five sons.

VICTORIA AND VENUS KING

(Great-nieces of Martin Luther King Jr.)

Victoria Chelsea King was born January 1, 1995, in Augusta, Georgia, to the late Rev. Vernon C. King and Minister Robin Scott-King. She currently resides in Greensboro, North Carolina, with her mother, who is youth pastor of their church, and her youngest sister, Venus Chantel King.

A high school honor student, Victoria is on the flag team and serves as the vice president of the youth ministry at her church. She is in the mime dance ministry holding the office of president, and is a Red Cross–licensed babysitter. She was crowned Mrs. Greensboro Professional Black Business Women's Queen in 2007, and Miss Black 2010 at Jamestown Middle School. She is a professional model and graduate of Barbizon School of Modeling in Atlanta, Georgia.

Victoria is a strong and compassionate young lady who understands that from those to whom much is given, much is required. She desires to be a model and doctor. She aspires to attend Spelman College and Harvard University. Her motto is "I am the best because God and my mommy said so!"

Venus Chantel King, the youngest daughter of Vernon C. King and Robin Scott-King, was born on October 31, 1998, in Lumberton, North Carolina. She lives in Greensboro, North Carolina, with her mother and sister, Victoria.

She is an honor student at her middle school, served as the volleyball team manager, and was a school office assistant. She is the treasurer for the youth ministry at her church and is in the mime dance ministry, holding the office of vice president. She also serves as the president of the youth media ministry.

Venus is a strong leader and plans to be a lawyer. She too aspires to attend Spelman College, and would like to go on to Howard University Law School. Her motto is "I will have the best because that's all I know!"

DEREK BARBER KING II AND KYLE KING
(Great-nephews of Martin Luther King Jr.)

Derek Barber King II was born in Atlanta, Georgia, to Derek Barber King and Janice Withers King. He attended schools in the Atlanta Public Schools system and graduated from Benjamin E. Mays High School. During high school, Derek developed an interest in culinary arts and decided to master his skills at the Le Cordon Bleu College of Culinary Arts in Atlanta. He graduated in May 2011.

Kyle Nelson Wendell King was born in West Palm Beach, Florida, to Derek Barber King and Janice Withers King. He is the younger brother of Derek Barber King II. Kyle attended Morehouse College and is currently enrolled in Gordon College, where he is studying sociology. Kyle is a gifted musician and athlete, as well as a model. The youngest male in the family with the King name, he is committed to keeping his uncle's dream alive.

INDEX

BASEBALL
SUPERSTARS ★ 2020

By K.C. Kelley

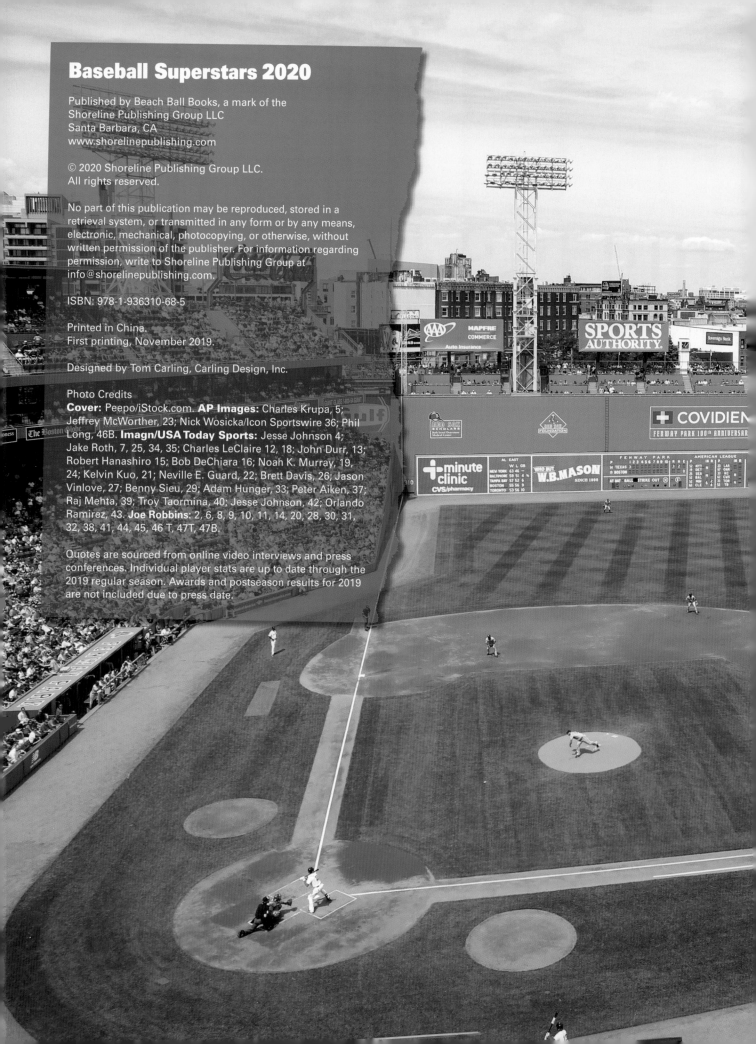

Baseball Superstars 2020

Published by Beach Ball Books, a mark of the
Shoreline Publishing Group LLC
Santa Barbara, CA
www.shorelinepublishing.com

ISBN: 978-1-936310-68-5

Printed in China.
First printing, November 2019.

Designed by Tom Carling, Carling Design, Inc.

Photo Credits
Cover: Peepo/iStock.com. **AP Images:** Charles Krupa, 5;
Jeffrey McWorther, 23; Nick Wosicka/Icon Sportswire 36; Phil
Long, 46B. **Imagn/USA Today Sports:** Jesse Johnson 4;
Jake Roth, 7, 25, 34, 35; Charles LeClaire 12, 18; John Durr, 13;
Robert Hanashiro 15; Bob DeChiara 16; Noah K. Murray, 19,
24; Kelvin Kuo, 21; Neville E. Guard, 22; Brett Davis, 26; Jason
Vinlove, 27; Benny Sieu, 29; Adam Hunger, 33; Peter Aiken, 37;
Raj Mehta, 39; Troy Taormina, 40; Jesse Johnson, 42; Orlando
Ramirez, 43. **Joe Robbins:** 2, 6, 8, 9, 10, 11, 14, 20, 28, 30, 31,
32, 38, 41, 44, 45, 46 T, 47T, 47B.

Quotes are sourced from online video interviews and press
conferences. Individual player stats are up to date through the
2019 regular season. Awards and postseason results for 2019
are not included due to press date.

CONTENTS

PLAY BALL!

If one thing can sum up the 2019 season, it would be the picture of a baseball flying out of a ballpark! The 2019 season was clearly "The Year of the Homer." MLB teams combined to hit an incredible 6,776 dingers. That was 671 more than the old record (which was set just two seasons ago!). What is going on? Some people think it is the baseball itself. Or was it the way more players are swinging for the fences? Strikeouts were up as well, after all. Whatever the reason, homers were the big story of the year. (See the box for more records.) Watch and see if the home run pace continues in 2020! Here were some other headlines from 2019:

The Bronx Bombers Are Back!

The New York Yankees have won more World Series than any other team, but their last one entering 2019 was way back in 2000. With a power lineup that looked like the Bombers of old, they bashed their way to an AL East title.

They Love LA!

The Dodgers won their seventh NL West title in a row. They started with a one-two pitching punch from Clayton Kershaw and Walker Buehler, along with new ace Hyun-Jin Ryu. But their big weapon was super-slugger Cody Bellinger, who became one of the NL's best all-around players.

Ready for Liftoff!

The Houston Astros continued their run amid the game's top teams. They won the whole thing in 2017 and threatened again in 2018. In 2019, they were neck-and-neck with the Yanks for top honors in the AL.

Young Sluggers

Amid all the home run heroics, the success of some rookies and young players stood out. Atlanta's Ronald Acuña Jr. became the second-youngest player ever with 30 steals and 30 homers. The Mets' Pete Alonso demolished the NL rookie record (and led the Majors) with 53 dingers. Houston's Yordan Álvarez only started playing in June but ended up

Nelson Cruz crushed 41 homers to help the Minnesota Twins set a new single-season team home run record.

with 27 homers! Cincinnati's awesomely named Aristides Aquino smacked 13 homers in August; that was tied for the most ever by a rookie in a month, and was also the most EVER in a player's first 100 times at the plate.

Family Ties!

Baseball has always been a family game. On the same day in 2019, two events showed why. First, Cavan Biggio of the Blue Jays hit for the cycle. His dad Craig had also done so, making them the second father-son team with a cycle. Then Giants OF Mike Yastrzemski hit a homer at Fenway Park, the same place his grandfather Carl was a Hall of Famer for 23 years with the Red Sox.

In 2020? Look for more homers, more young stars, and more baseball family stories. You're a part of that family, so thanks for reading!

Mike Yastrzemski greeted his grandpa, Carl "Yaz" Yastrzemski, before a game.

GOING! GOING! GONE!
Baseball Rewrites the Home Run Record Book

In 2019, MLB teams hit more homers than in any other season in history. When the dust settled, the 30 teams combined for a record number of long balls! Baseballs were flying out of the yard! Here's a wrap up of some of the other big, new, single-season home run records.

	RECORD
Most homers by a team	307, Minnesota Twins
Most homers by an NL team	279, Los Angeles Dodgers
Most homers by a league	3,478, AL
Most homers by an NL rookie	53, Pete Alonso, NY Mets
Most road homers by a team	170, Minnesota Twins
Most homers in a month by a team	75 (NY Yankees in August)
Most total homers in a month, all MLB	1,136 (August)
Most consecutive days with at least one two-homer hitter	37
Number of teams that set new team homer records	14
Most 30-homer seasons	58

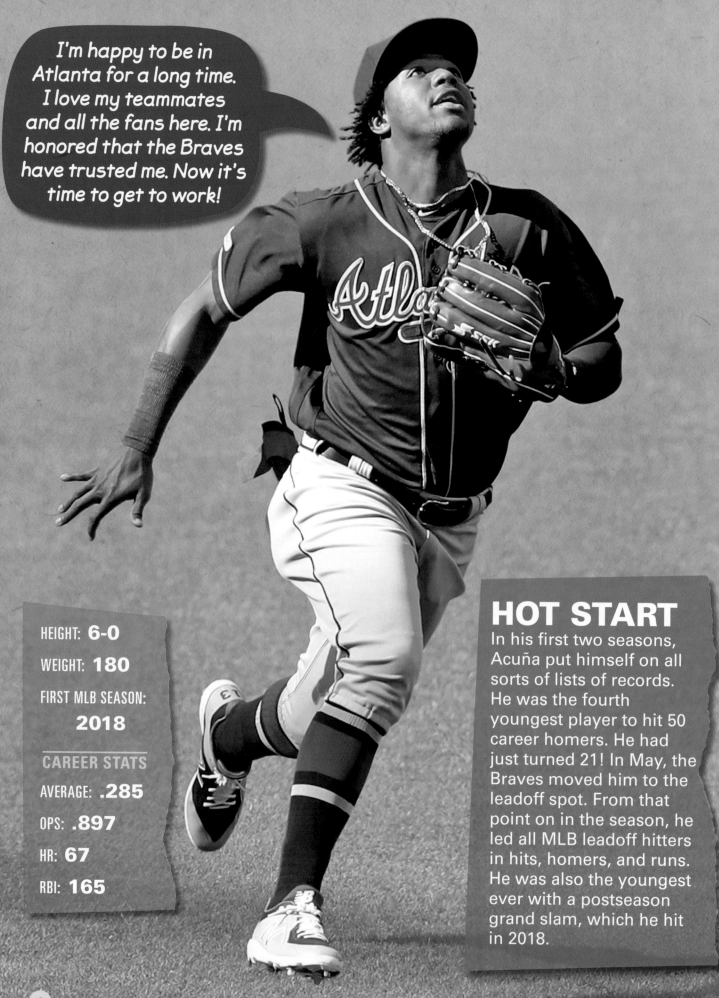

I'm happy to be in Atlanta for a long time. I love my teammates and all the fans here. I'm honored that the Braves have trusted me. Now it's time to get to work!

HEIGHT: **6-0**

WEIGHT: **180**

FIRST MLB SEASON: **2018**

CAREER STATS

AVERAGE: **.285**

OPS: **.897**

HR: **67**

RBI: **165**

HOT START

In his first two seasons, Acuña put himself on all sorts of lists of records. He was the fourth youngest player to hit 50 career homers. He had just turned 21! In May, the Braves moved him to the leadoff spot. From that point on in the season, he led all MLB leadoff hitters in hits, homers, and runs. He was also the youngest ever with a postseason grand slam, which he hit in 2018.

RONALD ACUÑA, JR.

Atlanta Braves ★ OUTFIELD

HOW DO YOU FOLLOW UP A ROOKIE-OF-THE-YEAR SEASON? BY HAVING A BETTER ONE! IN 2019, RONALD ACUÑA, JR., SHOWED THAT HE IS HERE TO STAY AMONG THE STARS!

ALL THE TOOLS!

Baseball experts talk about the five "tools" ballplayers need. Having three or four is usually enough. Ronald Acuña, Jr., has all five—and more! Hit for average? Better than .280, check. Hit for power? More than 60 homers in his two seasons, check. Run? He led the NL with 37 steals in 2019, check. Defense? He got Gold Glove votes, check. Throwing arm? That's 13 assists in two years, check. Five tools, five check marks. Watch and enjoy this young superstar continue to make his mark on the game.

DOUBLE THREAT

Few players combine speed and power like this young Braves star. In 2019, he became the second-youngest player ever with at least 30 homers and 30 steals in the same season. The youngest? A guy named Trout!

FAST FACT! Ronald comes from a baseball family in Venezuela. His dad played 8 seasons of minor league ball and his grandfather pitched!

NOLAN ARENADO

Colorado Rockies ★ THIRD BASE

HOME RUN POWER . . . HIGH AVERAGE HITTER . . . GOLD GLOVES EVERY YEAR. IS THERE ANYTHING NOLAN ARENADO CAN'T DO ON A BASEBALL FIELD?

MR. STEADY

You can't hit homers or snag ground balls if you're not in the lineup. Arenado has been one of the most dependable players in baseball. Since the 2015 season, he has missed fewer than 20 total games for the Rockies.

SOLID AS A ROCKIE!

How do you get to be as good as Nolan Arenado? Work, work, work. Though he's a five-time All-Star and has won the Gold Glove in each of his seven big-league seasons, Arenado takes nothing for granted. Hours before every game, he takes hundreds of swings, even in the elevator coming down from his apartment! Pregame infield practice drags on while Arenado asks for "one more." Away from the field, he watches hours of video—of baseball! He studies opposing pitchers as well as his own swing. The work paid off. He signed a contract for $260 million in 2019. Wow!

FAST FACT! Arenado racks up stats like few other hitters. He had at least 37 homers and 110 RBI each year from 2015 through 2019.

JAVIER BAEZ

Chicago Cubs ★ SHORTSTOP

JAVIER BRINGS A LOT OF GLOVES (SEE "BUSY GUY"), A POWER BAT, AND A TON OF POSITIVE ATTITUDE TO THE FIELD. THE RESULT? CHAMPIONSHIP!

BUSY GUY

Since becoming a full-time starter in 2016, Baez has needed a lot of gloves! His main position is shortstop, of course, but he has also helped out his team by playing second base, third base, and the outfield. What's next? Catcher?

CHAMPION CUBBIE!

Before the 2016 season, the Cubs put Javier Baez in as their starting shortstop. At the end of the season, Chicago had won its first World Series since 1908, and Baez was a big reason. His solid bat and great defense sparked the Cubbies time and again. As great as 2016 was for Baez and the Cubs, the 2018 season was even better for him. He led the NL with 111 RBI, a rare feat for a shortstop, hit a career-high .290, and finished second in the NL MVP voting. Beyond his baseball skills, Baez has become a key team leader.

FAST FACT! Baez has a great nickname: El Mago. That means "the magician" in Spanish. He earned it for his flashy glove work.

I get my passion for the game from when I was young, from playing with my brothers. That's how I try to play every day.

HEIGHT: **6-0**

WEIGHT: **190**

FIRST MLB SEASON: **2014**

CAREER STATS

AVERAGE: **.270**

OPS: **.794**

HR: **110**

RBI: **354**

WHAT A START!

When 21-year-old Javier Baez took the field for the Cubs in 2014, he was the youngest player in the Majors. He homered in his first three games— the first player since 1954 to do that! Chosen No. 9 in the 2011 MLB draft, Baez had grown up in Puerto Rico and gone to school in Florida before seeing his big-league dreams come true.

There's nothing like hitting a homer, like hitting a fastball flush on the bat. It's like an explosion off the bat!

HEIGHT: **6-4**

WEIGHT: **240**

FIRST MLB SEASON: **2016**

CAREER STATS

AVERAGE: **.265**

OPS: **.831**

HR: **78**

RBI: **287**

JOSH BELL

Pittsburgh Pirates ★ FIRST BASE

THE SLUGGING FIRST BASEMAN EMERGED IN 2019 AS ONE OF THE NATIONAL LEAGUE'S TOP POWER HITTERS. CAN HE CARRY THE PIRATES' OFFENSE IN 2020?

PITTSBURGH POWER!

Josh Bell knew he could hit. He had bashed 26 homers as a rookie in 2017. But pitchers figured him out, and he had trouble in 2018. Time for a change. He worked with his coaches to adjust his swing to create more lift. Boom! In 2019, his power emerged big-time and he became one of the leading extra-base hit machines in the league. He was in the top 10 in the NL in homers and doubles. And he helped his team by finishing sixth in the NL with 116 RBI. Bell's new power-packed swing has things looking up in Pittsburgh!

SWITCH!

Bell is unusual—a power-hitting switch-hitter. In 2017, his 26 homers set a National League record for rookies hitting from both sides of the plate. He hits most of his home runs right handed. And they go far: in 2019, he hit at least seven homers that each traveled at least 440 feet!

FAST FACT! Josh learned to stick with it. When he was 13, he was not accepted for a travel ball team. That just made him work harder!

CODY BELLINGER

Los Angeles Dodgers ★ OUTFIELD/FIRST BASE

AFTER A DISAPPOINTING WORLD SERIES, CODY BELLINGER RE-FOCUSED AND CAME OUT SWINGING IN 2019. THE RESULT? ONE OF THE BEST HITTING SEASONS IN YEARS!

MR. APRIL

In April 2019, Bellinger had one of the greatest months in baseball history. His 37 RBI, 47 hits, and 97 total bases were the most ever hit by May 1. His 14 homers tied for most in April!

BASEBALL BASHER!

Cody Bellinger can really hit. He set an NL rookie record with 39 homers in 2017 and was the league's Rookie of the Year. In 2018, he still did well, but the year ended badly for him, when he went 1-for-16 as the Dodgers lost the World Series. That just gave him fuel to have an outstanding 2019 season. Bellinger crushed the ball from Opening Day and finished with an incredible stat line: 47 homers, 115 RBI, and a .305 average. Bellinger's crushing uppercut swing was dialed in, and he came up with tons of clutch hits for another great Dodgers team.

FAST FACT! Is there anything Bellinger can't do on the baseball field? He'a a great slugger, but he can run, too. In 2019, he stole a career-best 15 bases.

HEIGHT: **6-4**		AVERAGE: **.278**
WEIGHT: **203**		OPS: **.928**
FIRST MLB SEASON: **2017**	CAREER STATS	HR: **111**
		RBI: **288**

> *My dad and I just love talking baseball. It's a blessing, I have a lot of great memories with him around the game.*

THANKS, DAD!

Cody had a built-in role model for his big-league dreams. His father, Clay, played for the Yankees and Angels. Clay also was a coach for Cody's Arizona youth team, which made it all the way to the 2007 Little League World Series. He didn't win, but it was a big first step for this future slugger.

I love working with the Jimmy Fund [the Red Sox children's charity]. We have so much but I think it's important to make sure to give back to them.

HEIGHT: **5-9**

WEIGHT: **180**

FIRST MLB SEASON: **2014**

CAREER STATS

AVERAGE: **.301**

OPS: **.893**

HR: **139**

RBI: **470**

RUN, RUN, RUN

That's what Mookie Betts's mom says he did as a kid—all the time! Betts grew up in Nashville and hit better than .500 in his final two high school seasons. He was a shortstop then, but moved to the outfield in the minors. Betts joined the Red Sox in 2014 and got a base hit in his first game at Yankee Stadium. And yes, he ran hard to first base!

MOOKIE BETTS

Boston Red Sox ★ OUTFIELD

BETTS WAS MR. EVERYTHING WHILE LEADING BOSTON TO THE CHAMPIONSHIP IN 2018. CAN HE AND THE RED SOX REBOUND TO WIN AGAIN IN 2020?

BETTS GOES TO WAR!

How good was Mookie Betts in 2018? He put together one of the best seasons in baseball history. While winning the AL MVP and leading Boston to a World Series title, Betts posted a 10.9 Wins Above Replacement (WAR) mark. This stat shows just how important a player was and how much he contributed. That 10.9 was the highest WAR score since 2001 and one of the top 20 highest ever! In 2019, Betts fell back a bit but remained among baseball's best players.

CHAMP!

Betts led Boston to its fourth World Series championship in the 2000s in 2018. He hit a home run in the clinching Game 5 win over the Los Angeles Dodgers. Betts and the team then enjoyed a long parade through the streets of Boston. They rode in "duck boats" that drove the streets on wheels and then took to the water for a Charles River cruise! Bonus Mookie trivia: He is one of the best bowlers in the Major Leagues!

FAST FACT! Betts is an all-around star with four 20-steal seasons and four Gold Gloves for his excellent defense.

ALEX BREGMAN

Houston Astros ★ THIRD BASE/SHORTSTOP

FIERY AND FIERCE, ALEX BREGMAN HAS EMERGED AS ONE OF THE BEST ALL-AROUND PLAYERS IN THE GAME— AND HE'LL BE HAPPY TO TELL YOU ABOUT IT!

CLUTCH

Bregman rises to the occasion. In the 2017 World Series, he smacked 2 homers and had 5 RBI. In all of his postseason games through the 2018 season, he had a total of 6 homers and 15 RBI.

WINNER, WINNER!

Since Alex Bregman a starting infielder for the Astros, the team has won 100 games in three straight seasons and took home the 2017 World Series title. That's no coincidence. Bregman's outstanding batting and solid defense combine with a fiery attitude to make him and Houston a winner. Bregman has improved in just about every category in his three full seasons. He blasted a career-high 41 homers in 2019 and spent most of the year amid the favorites for the AL MVP award. Even his defense improved, with his stats among the league's best.

FAST FACT! Among the many honors Bregman has earned was the 2018 All-Star Game MVP. He smack a lead-off homer in that game.

FILL-IN!

Bregman earned the respect of his teammates (and probably some MVP votes) when he moved from third to shortstop for more than 60 games in 2019. While replacing All-Star Carlos Correa, who was injured, Bregman kept up his power-packed hitting, while also committing only three errors at one of the game's toughest positions!

My confidence comes from putting pressure on myself in practice, so that you're ready for those moments when they come in a game.

HEIGHT: 6-0

WEIGHT: 180

FIRST MLB SEASON: 2016

CAREER STATS

AVERAGE: .286

OPS: .911

HR: 99

RBI: 320

COLLEGE MAN

After a great high school career in New Mexico (he set a state record with 19 homers as a junior), Bregman played three seasons at Louisiana State. In 2011, he was the national freshman of the year. In 2013, as a junior, he was named to several All-America teams while leading the Tigers to the College World Series championship. He was chosen by the Astros No. 2 in the draft that year—that's why he wears No. 2!

Making my Major League debut [in 2017] was a dream come true. I had been thinking about that day since the first time I played baseball.

HEIGHT: **6-2**

WEIGHT: **190**

FIRST MLB SEASON: **2017**

CAREER STATS

ERA: **3.68**

WHIP: **1.15**

WINS: **28**

LUIS CASTILLO

Cincinnati Reds ★ PITCHER

A BRIGHT LIGHT IN A DARK SEASON FOR THE REDS, LUIS CASTILLO HAS THE PITCHES AND THE POISE TO BECOME A SUPERSTAR IN CINCINNATI.

FUTURE STAR!

Being a winning pitcher on a team going through a tough season is hard. Luis Castillo solved that puzzle in 2019. His Cincinnati Reds finished six games below .500, but the young righty had one of the league's best records at 15–8. He also made his first All-Star Game. He had a high strikeout percentage and got hitters to pound out a lot of ground balls. He did have trouble with his control late in the season, but this young Dominican star has the skills and the attitude to rise to the top of the NL pitching ranks.

HEAT!

Baseball is overflowing with great strikeout pitchers these days. Castillo is right near the top of the heap. He finished 2019 with 226, good for ninth in the National League. Unlike some pitchers, he can get Ks with his great changeup, as well as blowing hitters away with a high-speed fastball.

FAST FACT! No, Castillo doesn't wear No. 42. He is shown here on the day when all players wear 42 to honor the great Jackie Robinson.

I'm so proud to put on the A's uniform and see all those people up there watching me play. I'm surrounded by people giving me so much support.

CITY KID

Davis is one of the success stories of a program by Major League Baseball to give more African American kids a chance to play ball. He grew up near the MLB Academy in Compton, California. He took part in baseball drills, played on teams there, and also worked on his studies. Davis became one of more than a dozen big-leaguers who have come from the Academy.

HEIGHT: **5-11**

WEIGHT: **203**

FIRST MLB SEASON: **2013**

CAREER STATS

AVERAGE: **.244**

OPS: **.815**

HR: **216**

RBI: **570**

KHRIS DAVIS

Oakland Athletics ★ DESIGNATED HITTER

THEY DON'T CALL HIM "KHRUSH" FOR NOTHING! A QUICK, POWERFUL HOME RUN SWING HAS TURNED DAVIS INTO ONE OF BASEBALL'S MOST RELIABLE LONG-BALL HITTERS.

KHRIS = KHRUSH!

Who led the Majors in home runs in 2018? Aaron Judge? Mike Trout? Christian Yelich? Nope, it was the Oakland slugger they call "Khrush!" Davis smacked 48 homers to continue a power rampage. From 2016 through 2018, in fact, no other player had as many dingers as Davis's 133. He also had three straight seasons with 100 or more RBI, including a career-best 123 in 2018. His totals fell off a bit in 2019 as he hit a long summer slump. But expect more big things from this Athletics slugger.

GO FOR TWO

In an era that has seen MLB players hit more homers than ever, Davis's power still stands out. From 2015 to 2019, he had 22 games with two or more homers. That was more than any other hitter in that time. In 2019, he was the first player to reach 10 homers for the year.

FAST FACT! After every one of his homers, Davis rounds second base before snapping off a salute to third base coach Ron Washington.

JACOB deGROM

New York Mets ★ PITCHER

IN A TIME WHEN HOME RUNS ARE FLYING MORE THAN EVER, JACOB DEGROM HAS MASTERED THE ART OF KEEPING THE BALL IN THE YARD—AND BECOME AN ALL-STAR!

LITTLE HELP?

DeGrom got every vote for the 2018 NL Cy Young Award even though he had a 10–9 record. How did that happen? His Mets teammates averaged only 3.5 runs in games he started, the lowest run support in the league. DeGrom's other stats earned him the award.

MR. QUALITY!

From mid-2018 to early 2019, Jacob deGrom put together an incredible streak. He went 26 games in a row with a quality starts—that means at least six innings pitched with three or fewer earned runs. That was an all-time record! Most of those helped him win the 2018 Cy Young Award, as did his sparkling 1.70 ERA. He kept it up in 2019, leading the NL with 255 strikeouts, and was second with a .978 WHIP (walks plus hits per inning pitched). How does he do it? Start with a 100-mph fastball and add in a wicked slider. That equals a record-setting pitcher!

FAST FACT! In his six seasons with the Mets, deGrom is already the team's all-time leader in WHIP and strikeouts per 9 innings.

My thing is to just focus on what I'm trying to do. I have my routines and I try to block out distractions. I just try to go out and do my job.

HEIGHT: **6-4**

WEIGHT: **180**

FIRST MLB SEASON: **2014**

CAREER STATS

ERA: **2.62**

WHIP: **1.05**

WINS: **66**

GOOD CALL

Believe it or not, deGrom was a shortstop in high school and college. While playing summer ball in 2009, he was told to be a pitcher. He quit the team instead! Fortunately for the Mets, he changed his mind and returned to pitch for Stetson University. By 2014, deGrom had made it to the Majors and was named the NL Rookie of the Year.

It's all about pitch selection. If you're swnging at good pitches to hit, you'll give yoursel a good chance to hit the ball hard. Try to lay off the pitcher's pitches and wait for yours.

HEIGHT: **6-3**

WEIGHT: **225**

FIRST MLB SEASON: **2011**

CAREER STATS

AVERAGE: **.292**

OPS: **.916**

HR: **243**

RBI: **807**

PAUL GOLDSCHMIDT

St. Louis Cardinals ★ FIRST BASE

ONE OF BASEBALL'S BEST ALL-AROUND PLAYERS WITH ARIZONA, GOLDSCHMIDT MOVED TO ST. LOUIS AND BROUGHT VETERAN PRESENCE AND AN ALWAYS-SOLID BAT.

WELCOME!

Goldschmidt made friends fast when he moved to St. Louis. In only his second game with the Cardinals, he blasted three home runs against the Milwaukee Brewers. That marked the first time in baseball history that a player hit that many in his first or second game with a new team!

QUIET SUPERSTAR!

Impress your friends by asking who were the only three players to be named an All-Star every year from 2013 to 2018. Mike Trout, of course. Royals catcher Sal Perez. And this guy—the silent superstar, Paul Goldschmidt. In eight seasons with Arizona, "Goldy" led the NL in homers, RBI, walks, slugging average, and on-base percentage. He won three Gold Gloves for his work at first base. He even had five seasons with 15 or more stolen bases! Arizona shocked its fans by trading this popular player to St. Louis before 2019.

FAST FACT! Another year, another 30 dingers— Goldschmidt smacked 34 homers in his first year with St. Louis.

Being able to fight alongside these guys day in and day out gives me the motivation to go out there and give it my all.

K MAN

A key pitching stat is strikeouts per 9 innings pitched. That is, if a pitcher threw a whole game, how many would he strike out? Hader doesn't have enough innings to qualify in this stat, but check this out— Max Scherzer led the NL in 2019 with 12.6. Hader's strikeouts per 9 innings pitched? An incredible 16.4!

HEIGHT: **6-3**

WEIGHT: **185**

FIRST MLB SEASON: **2017**

CAREER STATS

ERA: **2.42**

WHIP: **0.85**

SAVES: **49**

JOSH HADER

Milwaukee Brewers ★ PITCHER

DON'T BLINK OR YOU'LL MISS JOSH HADER'S NEARLY UNHITTABLE FASTBALL. THE TALL LEFTY PILES UP STRIKEOUTS AND SAVES LIKE FEW OTHER PITCHERS!

CLOSE THE DOOR!

Major League teams need a big, hard-throwing closer who can shut the door late in a game to preserve a win. Few pitchers have been as good at that as Josh Hader in the past couple of seasons. Blessed with a powerful fastball and a knee-knocking slider, Hader has rocketed up in just three seasons to be among baseball's best closers. In 2019, he averaged nearly two strikeouts per inning while racking up 37 saves for the Brew Crew. Hader struggled a bit in mid-2019 as batters began to adjust to his speed, but he found new life and new pitches and remains one of the best.

HAIRY!

Hader's long hair is almost as famous as his fastball. He's been wearing it very long for years. "I just don't like short hair," he says. It is so long that it once whipped across his face during a pitch and scratched his eye!

FAST FACT! During one stretch in 2018, Hader struck out 16 batters in a row. That was the longest such streak since 1969!

BRYCE HARPER

Philadelphia Phillies ★ OUTFIELD

EVERY TEAM IN BASEBALL WANTED TO GRAB THIS FORMER MVP FREE AGENT. THE PHILLIES WON THE PRIZE, AND HARPER KEPT UP HIS SLUGGING WAYS!

BIG MONEY

Before the 2019 season, fans everywhere wanted to know where Harper would land. Rumors flew around, and several teams made offers. Philly won by giving him an incredible 13-year contract that will pay him $330 million!

WORTH THE DOUGH!

Six All-Star teams, a Rookie of the Year trophy, and an MVP award. An all-around game that includes power and a rocket throwing arm. A reputation as a hard-nosed hustler. Put it all together and you've got Bryce Harper, one of the best all-around players in the game. He spent his first seven seasons with the Washington Nationals piling up long homers and dirty uniforms. The Nats made the playoff four times, but even Harper could not turn them into champs. He decided to move on after 2018, setting off a famous bidding war. Philadelphia fans are hoping to see more of the same great play from Harper!

FAST FACT! Harper set a career record in his first season as a Phillie, knocking in 114 runs. He also had his third 30-homer season.

As a team, we are so excited to come to the ballpark everyday and play in front of these great fans. We look forward to coming to the ballpark every day.

EARLY STAR

When Harper was only 16 years old, he was on the cover of *Sports Illustrated* magazine. The editors saw something special in the high school kid from Las Vegas. The pros agreed, but Harper could not jump from high school to the minors. Instead, he played a single season of community college ball in 2010. That summer, he was the No. 1 overall draft pick by the Washington Nationals. Two years later he was the Rookie of the Year!

HEIGHT: **6-3**

WEIGHT: **220**

FIRST MLB SEASON: **2012**

CAREER STATS

AVERAGE: **.276**

OPS: **.897**

HR: **219**

RBI: **635**

There's always something you can improve on. I wasn't satisfied with having just a great rookie year, I want to have lots of great years.

FAMILY

Judge grew up in north-central California. He and his brother were adopted by Wayne and Patty Judge. He was a high school football and baseball star. He chose Fresno State and baseball and starred for them for three seasons. He struggled early in the minors. At one point he had 42 strikeouts and only 4 homers!

HEIGHT: **6-7**

WEIGHT: **282**

FIRST MLB SEASON: **2016**

CAREER STATS

AVERAGE: **.273**

OPS: **.952**

HR: **110**

RBI: **246**

AARON JUDGE

New York Yankees ★ OUTFIELD

ALL RISE . . . TO WELCOME ONE OF BASEBALL'S MOST EXCITING YOUNG SLUGGERS. AARON JUDGE CARRIES ON A LONG YANKEES TRADITION OF POWER HITTERS.

SUPER POWER!

After seeing Aaron Judge hit four homers in a short visit to the Majors in 2016, few predicted what happened in 2017. The young slugger shocked Yankee Stadium and its loyal fans. He set a new Major League rookie record with 52 homers and finished second in the voting for the MVP award. He was just getting started. He reached 100 career homers in 2019 in only his 371st game, the third-fastest ever to that grand total. If he can battle back from some minor injuries, look for Judge to lay down the law again in 2020.

BIG AND TALL

Judge is not the tallest player ever at 6-7, or the heaviest at 280. But put them together and he is easily one of the overall largest Major League players ever. For a big guy, he moves well and has become an outstanding outfielder with a powerful throwing arm.

FAST FACT! Judge and the Yankees played Boston in a series in London, England. Judge smacked a homer in the first game!

Playing baseball is a kid's dream. We've always dreamed of putting on the uniform with a great organization and playing this game that we love.

HEIGHT: **6-3**

WEIGHT: **215**

FIRST MLB SEASON: **2012**

CAREER STATS

AVERAGE: **.279**

OPS: **.818**

HR: **207**

RBI: **598**

THE D.R.

Machado was born and raised in Miami, where he was a high school superstar. He was drafted third overall by the Orioles in 2010. After he became an MLB star, he chose to play for the Dominican Republic in the 2017 World Baseball Classic. His parents were both born on that island nation, and he wanted to honor them for their support of his career.

MANNY MACHADO

San Diego Padres ★ THIRD BASE/SHORTSTOP

THE PADRES WON THE BATTLE TO SIGN THIS ALL-AROUND STAR BEFORE THE 2019 SEASON. IS MANNY MACHADO THE KEY TO THE PADRES' PLAYOFF HOPES?

BIG MONEY

Machado was one of several top players who signed big deals before the 2019 season. When he got $300 million for 10 years from the Padres, it was the biggest contract in baseball history! Other players soon topped it, but that's how much the Padres knew they needed this big star.

MARVELOUS MANNY!

Manny Machado supplies big power from the hot corner and shortstop, a rare combination, indeed. The multi-talented infielder has posted one of the top 10 WAR scores of the past decade. In six-plus seasons with the Baltimore Orioles, he helped them reach the playoffs twice. He was traded during the 2018 season to the Los Angeles Dodgers, and his power bat helped them make it to the World Series. In his first season with San Diego, the four-time All-Star got his fifth career 30-homer season.

FAST FACT! Machado's trophy case includes a pair of Gold Gloves for fielding excellence. At the plate, led the AL with 51 doubles in 2013.

EDDIE ROSARIO

Minnesota Twins ★ OUTFIELD

EDDIE ROSARIO WAS AT THE CENTER OF MINNESOTA'S RECORD-SETTING HOMER CLUB IN 2019. IS HE READY TO TAKE THE TWINS BACK TO THE TOP?

OUT!

Rosario showed off his defensive skills in a big September win over Boston. With two outs in the ninth, he threw out Rafael Devers at home plate with a perfect throw from left field. It was the last out of the game!

HERE COMES EDDIE!

Eddie Rosario just keeps getting better and better. In 2019, he was a key part of the Twins' power surge, as the team set a new MLB record for homers. Rosario got off to a hot start, becoming the first Twins player ever with 10 homers before May 1. He kept slugging and ended with a career-high 32 homers. He also knocked in 109 runs, another new career best. Rosario brings high energy to the field along with his power bat and great outfield defense.

FAST FACT! Talk about a fast start! In 2015, Rosario swung at the first pitch in his first MLB at-bat . . . and hit a home run!

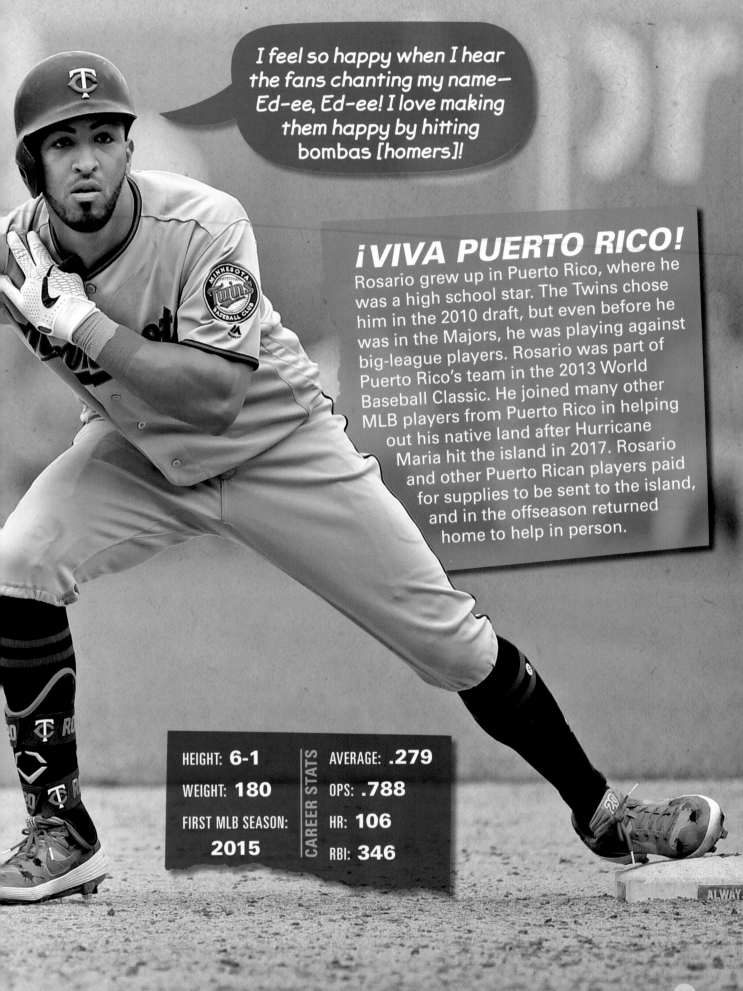

I feel so happy when I hear the fans chanting my name— Ed-ee, Ed-ee! I love making them happy by hitting bombas [homers]!

¡VIVA PUERTO RICO!

Rosario grew up in Puerto Rico, where he was a high school star. The Twins chose him in the 2010 draft, but even before he was in the Majors, he was playing against big-league players. Rosario was part of Puerto Rico's team in the 2013 World Baseball Classic. He joined many other MLB players from Puerto Rico in helping out his native land after Hurricane Maria hit the island in 2017. Rosario and other Puerto Rican players paid for supplies to be sent to the island, and in the offseason returned home to help in person.

HEIGHT: **6-1**

WEIGHT: **180**

FIRST MLB SEASON: **2015**

CAREER STATS

AVERAGE: **.279**

OPS: **.788**

HR: **106**

RBI: **346**

We're really good and we can play with everybody in this league. I know there are good teams, but we can compete with anyone out there.

HEIGHT: **6-3**

WEIGHT: **215**

FIRST MLB SEASON: **2008**

CAREER STATS

ERA: **3.20**

WHIP: **1.09**

WINS: **170**

MAX SCHERZER

Washington Nationals ★ PITCHER

THE PERFECT POWER PITCHER—MAX SCHERZER.
HE BEATS BATTERS WITH HIGH SPEED, WICKED CURVES,
AND FIERCE DETERMINATION!

MARVELOUS MAX!

Max Scherzer has been the best at just about every part of being a big-league pitcher. Win games? He has led the league four times. Strikeouts? Three-time league leader and averaging more than one per inning. Complete games? In a time when they are rare, Scherzer has topped the NL three times. The seven-time All-Star and three-time Cy Young winner (see box) has put together a Hall of Fame career . . . but he's not done. In 2019, Scherzer earned his second World Series appearance after reaching the playoffs seven times with two teams.

CY x 3!

Scherzer has been in the top 10 of the Cy Young voting every season since 2013. He was the award winner in 2013 with Detroit and in 2016 and 2017 with Washington, the fifth pitcher to win for both the AL and NL.

FAST FACT! Scherzer is famous among teammates for his intense dedication to studying hitters and his own pitching motion.

This season [2019] was the best I've ever felt offensively in the batter's box.

HEIGHT: **6-2**

WEIGHT: **235**

FIRST MLB SEASON: **2011**

CAREER STATS

AVERAGE: **.305**

OPS: **1.000**

HR: **285**

RBI: **752**

YOUNG TROUT

Trout followed in his father's footsteps. Jeff Trout had been a superstar at Millville (NJ) High School, where he set tons of baseball records. Along came Mike to break them all! Jeff left the coaching of his son to others, letting Mike just enjoy the game without pressure. That plan paid off as 17-year-old Mike was chosen by the Angels in the first round of the 2009 MLB Draft. One scout said, "He'll be in the Majors when he's 21." Nope. Mike made his debut at 19!